WHIZ BANG
WEB SITE F/X

WHIZ BANG
WEB SITE F/X

Written by Tom Lockwood
with Bray Jones

Whiz Bang Web Site F/X

Library of Congress Catalog No.: 96-71438

ISBN: 0-7897-0938-4

99 98 97   6 5 4 3 2 1

Interpretation of the printing code: the rightmost double-digit number is the year of the book's printing; the rightmost single-digit number, the number of the book's printing. For example, a printing code of 96-1 shows that the first printing of the book occurred in 1996.

"Screen reproductions in this book were created by using Capture from Mainstay, Camarillo, CA.," and Collage Plus from Inner Media, Inc., Hollis, NH.

Credits

PRESIDENT
Roland Elgey

PUBLISHER
Joseph B. Wikert

PUBLISHING MANAGER
Jim Minatel

TITLE MANAGER
Steven M. Schafer

EDITORIAL SERVICES DIRECTOR
Elizabeth Keaffaber

MANAGING EDITOR
Sandy Doell

DIRECTOR OF MARKETING
Lynn E. Zingraf

ACQUISITIONS MANAGER
Cheryl D. Willoughby

ACQUISITIONS EDITOR
Stephanie Gould

PRODUCT DEVELOPMENT SPECIALIST
Jácquelyn Mosley Eley

PRODUCTION EDITOR
Jim Bowie

PRODUCT MARKETING MANAGER
Kristine Ankney

ASSISTANT PRODUCT MARKETING MANAGERS
Karen Hagen
Christy M. Miller

STRATEGIC MARKETING MANAGER
Barry Pruett

TECHNICAL EDITOR
David Shinn
Tony Wasson

TECHNICAL SUPPORT SPECIALISTS
Mark Costlow
Nadeem Muhammed

ACQUISITIONS COORDINATOR
Jane K. Brownlow

SOFTWARE RELATIONS COORDINATOR
Susan Gallagher

EDITORIAL ASSISTANTS
Jennifer Condon
Andrea Duvall

BOOK DESIGNER
Ruth Harvey

COVER DESIGNER
Aaron Moore

PRODUCTION TEAM
Stephen Adams
Micheal Beaty
Wil Cruz
Trey Frank
Julie Geeting
Amy Gornik
Tammy Graham
Jason Hand
Daniel Harris
Casey Price
Erich Richter
Lisa Stumpf
Marvin Van Tiem

INDEXER
Cheryl Dietsch

Composed in *Century Old Style* and *Franklin Gothic* by Que Corporation.

To my wife, Dana, whose love and continued support made this effort possible and who makes life worth living.

About the Author

Tom Lockwood has 12 years experience as a technical writer and marketing specialist at Digital Arts, Advanced Graphic Solutions, Integrated Research, and Cinebase Software (all small but amazingly challenging and amusing places to work). His professional interests include HTML, Web page development, Internet education and anything else that is entertaining, obscure, or both. He is also a freelance writer. Tom is currently employed by Cinebase Software, the leaders in Digital Media Management Systems. He can be reached at **tlockwoo@cris.com** or via his personal Web site at **http://www.cris.com/~tlockwoo**.

Acknowledgments

Writing a book like this should be fun. And indeed it was. There are many people that had a hand in the creation of this book and I would like to thank them. Givon Strubble, although still a student at the University of Cincinnati, understands CGI scripting much better than I ever will; thanks Givon for your help on Chapter 15; it was invaluable. To George Menyhert, who introduced me to the folks at Que, I will always be indebted. To Bo Ferger and Cinebase Software, who let me take a week's vacation to finish this book. And thanks to Phil Beffrey at PIXAR, whose encouragement and friendship I've valued for more than 25 years; the lessons we learned in the early days of the computer-graphics industry are with me daily.

Additionally, there are several people at Que who deserve special thanks. Steve Schafer had the idea for this book and gave me the opportunity to write it. Stephanie Gould has been a kind and patient acquisitions editor, stretching deadlines whenever possible. Jim Bowie, thanks for your many corrections and suggestions. And a special thanks to Jacquie Eley, who read every word, made a multitude of suggestions, and kept me focused on the target of this book. Jacquie, I hope that you and the baby are doing well. The entire staff at Que was great as usual to work with.

We'd Like to Hear from You!

As part of our continuing effort to produce books of the highest possible quality, Que would like to hear your comments. To stay competitive, we *really* want you, as a computer book reader and user, to let us know what you like or dislike most about this book or other Que products.

You can mail comments, ideas, or suggestions for improving future editions to the address below, or send us a fax at (317) 581-4663. For the online inclined, Macmillan Computer Publishing has a forum on CompuServe (type **GO QUEBOOKS** at any prompt) through which our staff and authors are available for questions and comments. The address of our Internet site is **http://www.mcp.com** (World Wide Web).

In addition to exploring our forum, please feel free to contact me personally to discuss your opinions of this book: I'm **jeley@que.mcp.com** on the Internet.

Thanks in advance—your comments will help us to continue publishing the best books available on computer topics in today's market.

Jácquelyn Mosley Eley
Product Development Specialist
Que Corporation
201 W. 103rd Street
Indianapolis, Indiana 46290
USA

NOTE Although we cannot provide general technical support, we're happy to help you resolve problems you encounter that are related to our books, disks, or other products. If you need such assistance, please contact our Tech Support department at 800-545-5914 ext. 3833.

To order other Que or Macmillan Computer Publishing books or products, please call our Customer Service department at 800-835-3202, ext. 666. ■

Contents at a Glance

VIII | Appendixes

Table of Contents

8 GIF Animations Are Fun and Easy 113

9 Attract Attention with Dynamic Pages 133

IV | Sounds

10 Putting Audio on Your Web Page 151

VII | A Virtual Field Trip

16   Web Master's Bag of Tricks   235

17   Web Gallery   249

VIII | Appendixes

Introduction

Are you tired of developing and looking at the same old stuff on the World Wide Web? Do you wish you could create Web sites with finesse and pizzazz? Well, you can. There are many cool and powerful things you can do as a developer to make your Web site unique and exciting; just add a pinch of "whiz bang."

It seems like the latest and best stuff is scattered in a thousand places; well, it has been—that's why this book was written. This book contains whiz bang effects discovered in the archives of Netscape, unearthed from the bowels of Microsoft, and ferreted out of secret corners around the Internet.

Some things you can do include the following:

- Use style sheets to improve formatting.
- Create effective, clickable image maps.
- Use HTML tags to provide special effects.
- Add Shockwave and virtual reality to your pages.

- Create interactive and automatic Web pages.
- Create seamless, tiled backgrounds.
- Use cookies to store useful information about your visitors.
- And much, much more! ■

Who Should Use this Book?

Whiz Bang Web Site F/X is intended for anyone who has some experience creating Web pages, be they a hobbyist, personal Web page creator, or corporate intranet administrator who has a need or desire to create unique and exciting pages for display on the World Wide Web.

Of course, some HTML and graphic knowledge is assumed in this book, because the basics of Web publishing, including basic HTML, are not covered.

What You Will Find in this Book

In a nutshell, you will find tips, tricks, and traps of whiz bang Web sites for the following:

- Frames
- Images
- Backgrounds
- Clickable image maps
- GIF animation
- Audio
- Shockwave
- Multimedia
- Java
- CGI scripts

The last chapter of the book contains a gallery of whiz bang Web sites as a special treat!

Features Used in this Book

This book contains various features to make it easier to use.

Chapter Road Maps

Each chapter begins with a brief introduction and a list of the topics you'll find covered in that chapter. You know what you'll be reading about from the start.

Visual Aids

Notes, Tips and Cautions give you useful information throughout the book. The following are descriptions of each element.

N O T E Notes provide useful information that isn't essential to the discussion. They usually contain more technical information, but can also contain interesting but nonvital technical or nontechnical information. ▪

 T I P Tips reveal hints and tricks that will enhance your Web-site experience.

CAUTION

Cautions warn you against actions that could cause you problems or take the whiz bang out of your site.

The CD-ROM

Inside the back cover of this book, you'll find a CD-ROM containing multi-megabytes of links, tips, and programs to help you get the most for your whiz bang buck.

The Web

## CHAPTER 1

The Newest, Brightest, and Best—A Quick Tour

You begin this book by taking a breakneck tour around the Internet. Who's making the most noise? Who's pushing the envelope? And, maybe most importantly, who's providing the tools that allow mere mortals to have fun creating Web sites and add nifty things to them? That's really what this book is all about. It's designed so that all you have to do is thumb through it, see something you like, and plug it into your Web page. You will find a concentration on things that you can do with a text editor and shareware paint applications (if you have more expensive software, great, but most of the really nifty stuff is shareware anyway).

There is also a concentration on things you should avoid. Sometimes, the best thing you can do is avoid doing something painful. So watch for the Cautions. ■

How best to implement tables, frames, and style sheets

Plain text doesn't have to be so plain anymore, and with the inclusion of style sheets you can get some truly fantastic formatting that requires almost no work.

Greatest graphic goodies

What's the best way to put animation on a page? When should you use which image format? These and other graphic gems revealed.

Astounding audio

Put MIDI, AIFF, and AU audio on your Web page today. Add controls so your clients can adjust the volume, pause, and stop the audio.

A peek behind the scenes

How can you create interactive and automatic Web pages? Well, you'll get CGI scripts and Java applets galore to plug in and play with.

A treasure trove of goodies

You'll see the best shareware applications available. Having these products on the CD will literally save you days of download time.

Part II—Plain Text

Plain Text with Pizzazz

All right already, more text stuff? Yes, but only the latest extensions and features are covered here (see Figure 1.1), such as how to create multiple-column documents without tables, how to specify exact font faces by name, and how to use the most revolutionary addition to the HTML specification—the cascading style sheet (CSS).

FIG. 1.1
Become familiar with style sheets; in the not too distant future they'll change the way you format documents for the Web.

Using Tables Effectively

Tables help you organize data and create documents that cry out for formatting. But are tables always the way to go? Are they overused? How can you use them most effectively? In the tables chapter you will lay out a newsletter, as demonstrated in Figure 1.2—something that you might actually need to do. You can use tables in many ways; this chapter contains enough detail and step-by-step instruction that you should be an expert by the time you're done.

FIG. 1.2
This newsletter is a great example of just how versatile tables can be.

Using Frames Effectively

Frames are misunderstood and way underused. If you want to present information to your end users in a well-organized, effective way, you should learn how to implement frames. One very nice feature is the way frames naturally fit into the model used by browsers, letting you create buttons that target other windows. In this example, we look at an interactive music catalog. See Figure 1.3.

FIG. 1.3
With the ability to nest frames and hide their borders, you can quickly put together interactive documents.

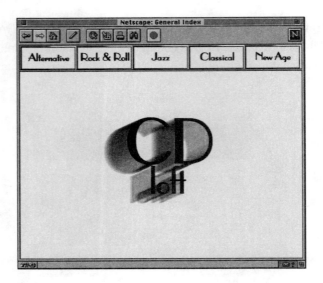

Part III—Sights

Cool Effects with Images

Here you find all the information you need to make a good choice for image file formats. Should you use GIF or JPEG to present an image such as Figure 1.4? How about PNG and Waveletts, Progressive JPEG? In addition, you will find some nice graphic tricks that let you minimize image download time and provide special effects.

Time for a Background Check

You learn the following: how to create your own seamless, tiled backgrounds; how to make it look like foreground elements are casting shadows on your backgrounds; how to create a shelf along the left edge of your window, as in Figure 1.5; why you should seriously consider using solid colors as backgrounds; and dos and don'ts for using backgrounds.

FIG. 1.4
It's all about minimizing image size and improving performance.

FIG. 1.5
You can use backgrounds as a means to separate main text from an index portion of your page.

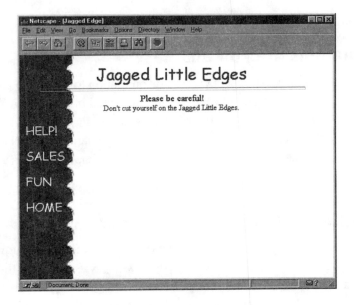

Getting the Most from Clickable Image Maps

Clickable image maps, like the one in Figure 1.6, add so much interaction to your Web pages that you may be considered dangerous after reading this chapter. You not only see how to put together a functional image map, but you also receive all of the tools you need to do so.

FIG. 1.6
The Polish have had a tough couple of decades. Hey, at least their borders haven't changed.

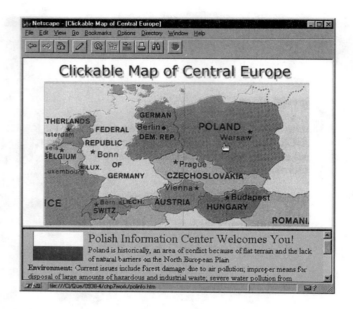

GIF Animations Are Fun and Easy

GIF animations are the best way to add animation to your Web pages and can be used in many ways, one of which is demonstrated in Figure 1.7. You hear from the king of GIF Animation, Mr. Bray Jones, who reveals his secret tips and tricks for creating these cool effects. This is not simply a chapter about the GIF format or about using the IMG tag more effectively. This chapter alone is well worth the price of this book.

Attract Attention with Dynamic Pages

If GIF doesn't fit your fancy, we've provided other means for putting animations on your pages. Scroll text across your pages with JavaScripts and the <MARQUEE> tag, as in Figure 1.8. Learn how to use CGI scripts and Java applets for animations. Also, create documents that automatically download to your clients every second, minute, or day, or put a self-running demo or slide show together.

FIG. 1.7
Here, text is being "painted" on the screen by using a GIF animation.

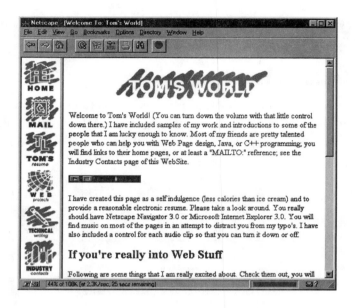

FIG. 1.8
Scrolling text is easier to implement than it is to read. Be careful where you use some of these top secret effects.

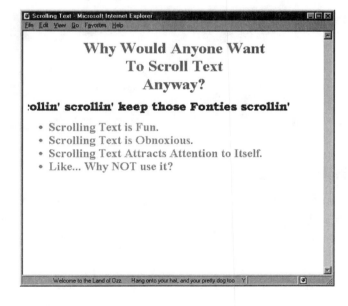

Part IV—Sounds

Putting Audio on Your Pages

This chapter takes a no-nonsense approach to getting audio on your page in a hurry. What tag should you use? If background MIDI tracks aren't enough, create an audio library where folks can control the volume, pause, and can stop your audio segments. See Figure 1.9.

FIG. 1.9
There are some scripting examples here that are easy to implement and will floor visitors to your site.

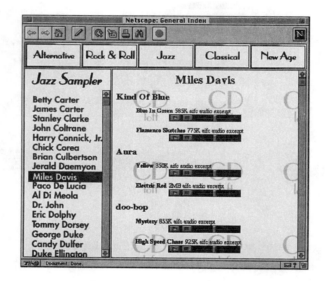

Working with Audio

Here you find out how to edit audio so that it is more usable on your Web site. See Figure 1.10. This chapter also makes a great reference for audio formats, play rates, and file size. Need to know how to get the most sound for your download dollar? You'll find it here.

FIG. 1.10
Learn how to tweak
audio so that it
soothes the soul.

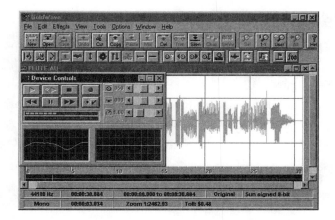

Part V—Multimedia

All that Shockwave

Find out what makes Shockwave tick, as in Figure 1.11. Is it the answer to your
prayers? You won't just see screen shots, but you get a CD demo so you can get
a good look at its capabilities and a feel for how it works.

FIG. 1.11
Will Shockwave solve
your problems or will
it give you sticker
shock? Find out in
this chapter.

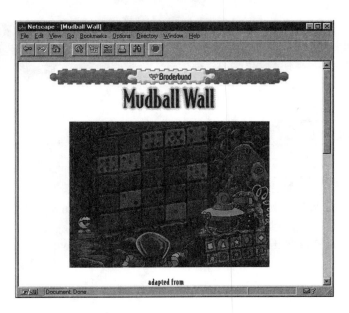

Making the Most of Multimedia

MPEG, QuickTime VRML, and VRML 2.0. These are some of the biggest buzz words on the Net. Why? Because each possesses tremendous potential for the future. See Figure 1.12. In this chapter, you will learn enough about this technology so that you can put your own virtual world on your home page (OK, maybe you will put somebody else's virtual world on your Web page). Anyway, you should check out these technologies so that you are ready for the next revolution to sweep the Net.

FIG. 1.12
New York City. Gosh it's gotten a lot cleaner since the last time I was there.

Part VI—Behind the Scenes

Java, Cookies, and Other Tricks

Java is... You fill in the blank. There is a lot of hype surrounding Java, but what it comes down to is that this little programming language could change the way most of us use computer and software applications, as shown in Figure 1.13. We've provided the Java Developer's Kit (JDK) on the CD for both Windows machines and

Macintoshes. The JDK is not only a tool for programmers; it includes a bunch of applets that you can customize for your needs.

FIG. 1.13
Even scientists find
Java fun and useful.

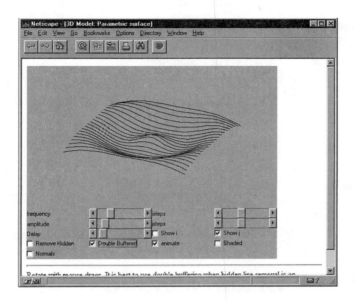

CGI Scripts

CGI scripts can provide a host of solutions to your Web-site needs. Need a Guest Book? A counter? A message board? A search engine? Or a currency converter, as shown in Figure 1.14? The list goes on. This chapter introduces you to each of these scripts and gives you a quick tutorial on script configuration. Then, on the accompanying CD, you find these scripts hand brewed for you at Matt's Script Archive. These scripts are another "must have" on this CD. Again, no programming necessary.

FIG. 1.14
CGI scripts aren't always pretty, but they do provide important features for you and your clients.

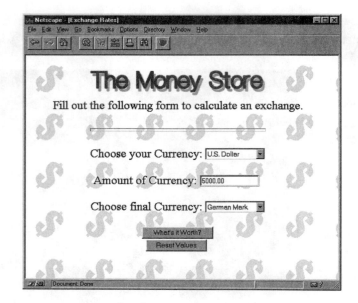

Part VII—A Virtual Field Trip

Bag of Tricks

Need an HTML editor, Plug ins, a good paint package, CGI scripts, Java applets, example files, or utility programs? This is the place to look. The best shareware and freeware around has been assembled on this CD, like the HTML editor in Figure 1.15. Now, you can fire this stuff up without waiting for those big, old files to download.

HTML tag palette

FIG. 1.15
If you've never worked with a sophisticated HTML editor, here's your chance to test drive one.

HTML edit window

Preview window

Tool palettes

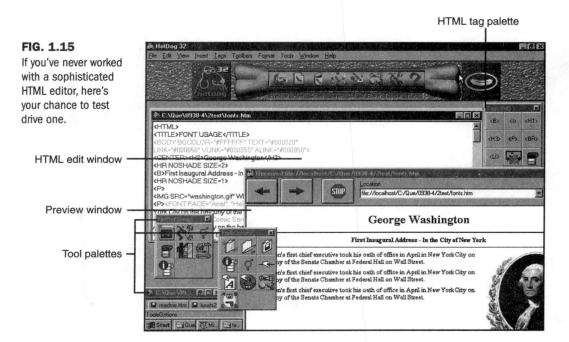

Web Gallery

You get a look at the best on the Net with a "Web Gallery." Here, you find the latest technologies, the most exciting content, and the most useful tools.

While researching this book, I have gotten even more excited and interested about the Internet. It's a wonderful technology, and it's not so complicated that people like us will get lost while trying to plug in a few new features. Good luck on your wild ride! I hope you enjoy this book.

Plain Text

Plain Text
with Pizzazz

It used to require tables, frames, and other HTML trickery to get good-looking Web pages. However, better looking documents are now available through new methods being used by HTML, Netscape Navigator, and Internet Explorer extensions. ■

Create multicolumn documents

This used to be difficult; now simply use the MULTICOL tag and its attributes to create multicolumn documents.

Space text easier

The SPACER tag will be great for implementing tabs, indents, and other types of vertical and horizontal spacing.

Define particular fonts

Now you can tell the browser that you want it to use Helvetica Bold or Book Antigua.

Use the new HTML cascading style sheets (CSS)

These are not particularly easy to hand code. But, they do hold the promise of making HTML look a lot more like something you'd expect from a desktop-publishing application.

Creating Multicolumn Documents

There are a series of Netscape extensions that let you create multicolumn documents easily. You no longer need to use tables and frames to get text to flow from one column to another. The beauty of these tags is that they work very consistently when your browser is resized. You can set specific sizes for your columns or let their width be controlled by the size of the browser window.

Implementing the Multicolumn Tag

The multicolumn tag, MULTICOL, enables you to set the number of columns, the column's width, and the space between the columns (gutter).

The following line creates a multicolumn section, two columns wide, each column of which is 200 pixels wide, with a 25 pixel gutter between them.

```
<MULTICOL COLS=2 WIDTH=200 GUTTER=25>
```

The MULTICOL tag can be inserted anywhere within a document. It must be closed with a MULTICOL tag, or all text will appear in a single column in what should be the left column.

The following is an excerpt from the HTML used to create Figure 2.1:

```
... received the second greatest number of votes.
<P>
<MULTICOL COLS=2 GUTTER=25>
<SPACER TYPE=HORIZONTAL SIZE=25><I>Fellow-Citizens of the Senate and
➡of the House of Representatives: A<font size="-1">MONG</font> the
➡vicissitudes ...</I>
</MULTICOL>
On the other hand, the magnitude and difficulty of the trust to which
➡the voice of my country ...
```

FIG. 2.1
You can create multiple-column documents like this by using the Netscape tag MULTICOL.

Spacer tag used as a tab

Spacer tag used to add vertical white space

Multiple columns

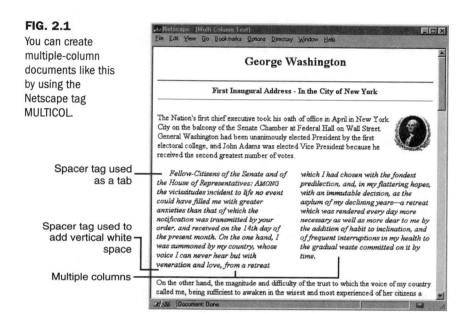

Part

II

Ch

2

Multicolumn Facts

The following is a series of facts about the MULTICOL tag:

- MULTICOL tags can be nested.
- The MULTICOL tag has no effect on styles assigned by the FONT tag.
- If column widths are not explicitly set, they grow to fit the browser window.
- Columns, unlike table cells, do not expand to make room for elements that may be too large to fit. So, if you place an image in a column that is naturally too large to fit, it will "flow over" into the adjoining column.

CAUTION

At the time this book was published, only Netscape Navigator supported these column tags. Because these features only modify text to make it more legible, the files will still be viewable in browsers that do not support the MULTICOL tag. If most of your audience will not be using Navigator 3.0 or later, do not bother using this tag. Figure 2.2 shows what this document looks like in a browser that does not support the MULTICOL tag.

FIG. 2.2
This document, when viewed with Internet Explorer, is still legible, but the formatting is not nearly as effective. Compare this with Figure 2.1.

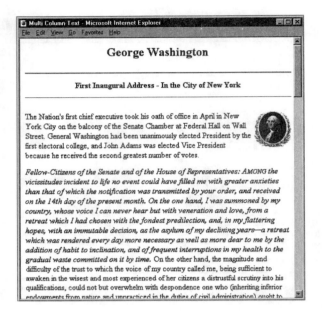

The SPACER Tag

Another Netscape extension is the SPACER tag. In the simplest sense it lets you simulate a tab of a certain width. Figures 2.1 and 2.3 demonstrate the effect of the following tag in the first line of the multicolumn section.

```
<SPACER TYPE=HORIZONTAL SIZE=25>
```

The above command creates a horizontal space. SPACER also lets you add vertical white space. The following line is an example:

```
<SPACER TYPE=VERTICAL SIZE=50>
```

This command places a 50-pixel vertical white space in the document.

> **CAUTION**
>
> As with the MULTICOL tag, SPACER is a Netscape Navigator extension and is not supported by other browsers at this time.

Explicitly Specifying Fonts

You can now specify which particular fonts you want displayed in your documents. Of course, it depends on the clients' systems having the fonts that you specify.

Specifying the Font FACE

The attribute that you use to specify a font type is the FACE attribute, an attribute of the FONT tag, and is used as follows:

```
<FONT FACE="font name", "second choice", "third choice">
```

It is important that you are careful when specifying the font name. It must be spelled correctly, with appropriate spaces; and you must remember these names are case sensitive. As in the following example, you will normally want to specify one font name for Windows systems and a second font name for Macintosh systems. The results of explicitly specifying fonts, as demonstrated in the following HTML, can be seen in Figure 2.3.

```
<P><FONT FACE="Arial", "Helvetica">The Nation's first chief executive
➥took his oath of office in April in New York City on the balcony of
➥the Senate Chamber at Federal Hall on Wall Street.</FONT>
➥<P><FONT FACE="Comic Sans MS", "Parisian">The Nation's first chief
➥executive took his oath of office in April in New York City on the
➥balcony of the Senate Chamber at Federal Hall on Wall Street.</
➥FONT> <P>The Nation's first chief executive took his oath of office
➥in April in New York City on the balcony of the Senate Chamber at
➥Federal Hall on Wall Street.
```

N O T E Microsoft provides a series of fonts that you can download. These are available at its Web site. These fonts can be downloaded for Macintosh and Windows operating systems. Of course, you may not have control over which of these fonts your users have loaded. ■

FIG. 2.3

The first two paragraphs in this figure show the results of explicitly assigning the fonts "Arial" and "Comic Sans MS."

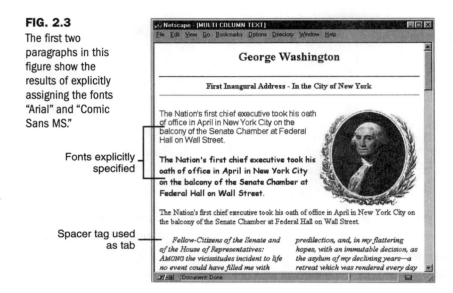

Fonts explicitly specified

Spacer tag used as tab

If the browser does not find the font specified, the default font for the browser is used.

Creating Underline and Strikeout Fonts

Two new tags let you create underlined and strikeout text. They are <S> and <U>. These tags have been used to create the text in Figure 2.4. These attributes are used as follows.

```
<P>It's not spelled <S>Potatoe</S>
<P>It's spelled <U>Potato</U>!
```

FIG. 2.4
The strikeout and underline tags are supported by Netscape Navigator and Internet Explorer.

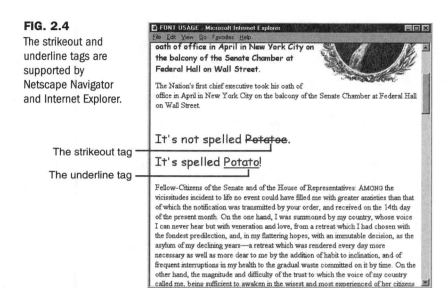

The strikeout tag
The underline tag

The New Super Tool—Cascading Style Sheets

Get used to hearing about style sheets. They are extremely powerful devices used to control text and image placement. With a style sheet you can define a font's face and weight, interline spacing, color, and indentation; in short, you will finally have the same controls over HTML as you would expect to find in a desktop-publishing application. If you've used Microsoft Word's Style Sheets or FrameMaker's Paragraph Catalog, you are already familiar with the power and freedom that style sheets afford.

For detailed information, see the W3 site for a complete specification (**www.w3.org/pub/WWW/TR/WD-css1.html**).

You can add style sheets to your documents by doing the following:

- Include style commands within the body of your HTML documents.

  This is a quick and easy way to do things like specify margins for a block of text.

- Include or embed a style sheet before the <BODY> tag in your HTML document.

  This method can provide powerful control over all tags in your document, simultaneously. The only disadvantage of this method is that the styles specified in the document are not applied to any other documents.

- Link to external style sheets.

  Using this method, you can modify the appearance of a group of documents by changing one style sheet.

As the popularity of style sheets grow, they will obviously be set by application programs that let you use pull-down menus and other text and page formatting GUIs. For now, you may want to get familiar with these sheets. By simply including a couple of commands to control your most common tags like H1, H2, H3, LI, P, and Body, you can radically improve the appearance of your document. In this section, we do not try to define or explain the CSS specification but rather show a couple of quick examples of what, no doubt, will become the most important method for controlling the appearance of HTML documents.

What the Style Sheet Looks Like

Styles are made up of HTML tags followed by the properties that you assign to them. For example:

```
H2 {font-size: 18pt;
font-weight: bold;
color: blue}
```

The above specifies that all <H2> tagged paragraphs will appear as 18-point, bold, blue text. This code works regardless of the manner that it is applied. That is, this code can appear in the body of a document, before the body of the document, or as a linked style sheet. There are many, many style attributes; you will want to consult the W3 document, as well as the Microsoft and Netscape Web sites for implementation details.

> **CAUTION**
>
> At the time of this writing only Microsoft Internet Explorer supports style sheets. Their implementation is not complete. The examples that follow use conventions that are recommended and have been tested with Explorer. Netscape Navigator has announced style sheet support for the next release (Netscape Navigator 4.0); will there be differences or conflicts? Probably, but because style sheets have been specified by W3C any incompatibility issues should be handled rather quickly.

Part
II
Ch
2

Inline Styles

You can place style commands in the Body of an HTML document for control on a paragraph-by-paragraph basis. For example:

```
<H1 STYLE="margin-left: 0.5in; margin-right: 1.0in">
```

Creates a H1 text that is indented .5 inches from the left margin and 1 inch from the right margin.

With this implementation the next H1 tag will not be indented. It will be a normal, default H1 tag. In this example, that entire chunk of code was used to modify only one line of text. That's an awful lot of work for little effect. However, if you do want exact control of text layout, style sheets can be used on a character-by-character basis to modify the appearance of your pages.

Embedding a Style Block

You can place a style block before the BODY tag. By placing the style block here the style defined will be applied to all tags in the rest of the document. By embedding style blocks you can change everything about the way your page looks. For example, you could create a version of your page that is designed for seniors with very conservative, large fonts, and traditional background treatments. What happens when you link to this document from MTV? Just make a copy of this document, put it in a different directory and modify the style block in the Head of your page. Text can now be pink and orange on a flowered background. Style sheets allow these simple global changes for dramatically different effects. The style sheet in the Listing 2.1 was used to create the HTML document in Figure 2.5.

Listing 2.1   Sample of a style sheet

```
<HTML>
<head>
<TITLE>Keats, John. 1884. Poetical Works.</TITLE>
<STYLE  TYPE="text/css">
<!--
BODY  { background: white;
     color: black;
     font-size: 80%; }
P  { color: black;
     font-size: 80%;
     margin-left: 15%;
     margin-right: 20%;
     font-family: Verdana, Arial, Helvetica, helv, sans-serif }
H1, H2, H3 { font-size: 180%;
     margin-left: 10%;
     margin-right: 20%;
     font-weight: medium;
     color: coral;
     font-family: Comic Sans MS, Arial, Helvetica, helv, sans-serif }
.descript { color: silver;
     margin-left: 10%;
     margin-right: 10%;
     font-family: Verdana, Arial, Helvetica, helv, sans-serif }
A:link  { color: coral;
     font-weight: bold;
     text-decoration: none; }
A:visited  { color: purple;
     font-weight: bold;
     text-decoration: none; }

.topline {color: silver;
     margin-left: 10%;
     margin-right: 10%;
     font-size: 80%;
     font-family: Verdana, Arial, Helvetica, helv, sans-serif }
-->
</STYLE>
</HEAD>z
<BODY>
Body text goes here!
</BODY>
</HTML>
```

Take a look at the syntax. If you are familiar with HTML, there is nothing here that is really the least bit complicated.

The only difference between the HTML documents in Figure 2.5 and Figure 2.6 is the style sheets that are assigned to them. Once you have a couple of style sheets defined you can use them by cutting and pasting them or by linking your documents to them. Although a little bit of work to create, they certainly are nicer than using all those FONT, B, I, and BLOCKQUOTE tags that don't always do the job.

FIG. 2.5
Style sheets let you modify a page's attributes quickly and globally.

FIG. 2.6
With only slight modifications to style sheets you can get a completely different look. Please compare this with Figure 2.5.

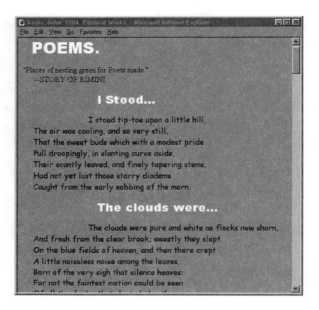

Linking to Style Sheets

In the previous section, embedded style sheets were shown. However, if you make a change to your style sheet, you might want to change a series of similar documents. In that case, opening each document and making the change would be inconvenient, error prone, and a waste of your time. So, you can link to style sheets with a command similar to the one that follows:

```
<HEAD>
<TITLE>Horton Hears A What?</TITLE>
<LINK REL=STYLESHEET HREF="http://www.name.com/yourstyle.css"
➥TYPE="text/css">
</HEAD>
```

These style sheets will contain the same commands as those specified in the "embedded" example earlier in this chapter. The styles are applied exactly the same way whether they are embedded or linked.

TIP   Use the <!– tag to make these style sheets invisible in browsers that do not support style sheets. Otherwise, you may have chunks of style sheet commands appearing where you don't want them.

Where to Go From Here?

- Chapter 3, "Using Tables Effectively"

  To learn how to place text in tables.

- Chapter 4, "Using Frames Effectively"

  To learn how to use frames as a powerful organizational and text-formatting mechanism.

- **www.w3.org/pub/WWW/TR/WD-css1.html**

  For more information about CSS (cascading style sheets), see the W3C site.

Using Tables Effectively

Tables were originally introduced to HTML as a way to organize text in a tabular fashion. However, HTML (particularly the earliest versions) provides very poor page-layout capabilities. So, every tag that provided any control over text and graphics was quickly employed to make documents look more interesting.

Tables are still really good for storing text and numbers. In this chapter, we go beyond the standard use of tables and stretch them as far as we can. Let's start with the example of designing a newsletter, as seen in Figure 3.1. This is a good example because it not only points out the strength of the table tag but also demonstrates its weaknesses. ■

Assuring exact image alignment

In some cases, exact image alignment is critical so that you do not see discontinuity (seams) across image boundaries.

Using a table as a spacer

You can use tables as invisible spacers to separate graphical elements or to separate graphical elements from visible tables.

Specifying exact table width

Fitting images and text together neatly is a challenge, but you'll find some helpful hints here.

Using nested tables

You can put tables inside of tables, creating sophisticated visual effects and useful navigational blocks.

Coloring individual cells

Now, you can change the color of each cell, which really helps to draw the reader to a specific area.

Using a transparent image for spacing

You can create a fully transparent GIF image and scale it to any size to create white space as you need it.

FIG. 3.1
A newsletter provides many challenges for the Web-page designer.

Assuring Exact Image Alignment

In the upper left corner of the newsletter we have a case where the masthead and sidebar meet. See Figure 3.2. It is critical that these two images align exactly, because they were cut from the same large image with a patterned background. If alignment is off by one pixel, a line will be visible where the images meet. Rather than using a table, it is easier to align the images before you start the TABLE tag.

Notice in the following HTML example that "BORDER=0".

```
<IMG SRC="pics/masthead.jpg" HEIGHT=75 WIDTH=508 BORDER=0><BR>
<IMG SRC="pics/sidebar.jpg" HEIGHT=480 WIDTH=75 BORDER=0 ALIGN=LEFT
HSPACE=0>
<TABLE ... etc.
```

FIG. 3.2
If one pixel is off, you will see a very visible line across the "seam" of these images.

Critical region for alignment, potential seam

Sidebar image

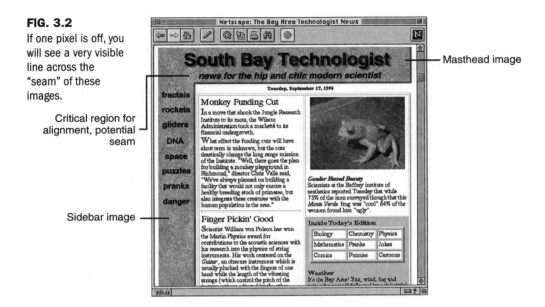

Masthead image

Using a Table as a Spacer

The date directly below the masthead is a one-row, one-cell table, as you can see in Figure 3.3. You could use an image here as a spacer; however, the date of this newsletter will change frequently, making a table the perfect choice as a spacer, and as a location to display the date.

Following is the HTML that created the table spacer and date holder displayed in Figure 3.3.

```
<TABLE BORDER=0 WIDTH=425 CELLPADDING=2>
<TR><TD ALIGN="CENTER"><FONT SIZE="-1"><B>Tuesday, September 17, 1996
</B></FONT><BR></TD></TR>
</TABLE>
```

Part

II

Ch

3

FIG. 3.3

Don't be afraid to use tables in nonstandard ways (as a one-cell spacer and date holder in this example), particularly when they contain text that you want to modify periodically.

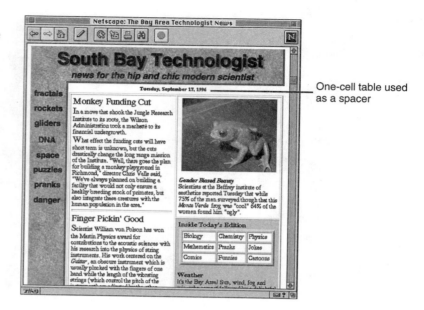

One-cell table used as a spacer

Nesting Tables

The "Inside Today's Edition" heading is followed by a table of contents. See Figure 3.4. This table of contents is, appropriately, a table. As long as you know where in the HTML to insert the new table tag the process is straight forward.

```
<TR>
<TD HEIGHT="200" VALIGN=TOP BGCOLOR="#DEDE9C">
<FONT SIZE=4><B>Inside Today's Edition</B></FONT><BR>
<CENTER>

<TABLE WIDTH=190 CELLPADDING="2" CELLSPACING="3" BORDER="3">
<TR>
<TD WIDTH=60 BGCOLOR="#FFFFFF">Biology</TD>
<TD WIDTH=60 BGCOLOR="#FFFFFF">Chemistry</TD>
<TD WIDTH=60 BGCOLOR="#FFFFFF">Physics</TD>
  .
  .
  .
</TD>
</TR>
</TABLE>

</TD>
</CENTER>
</TR>
```

FIG. 3.4
Here a table is used
to list a series of
elements later in the
publication. Notice
how its borders and
colors are different
from the table in
which it is nested.

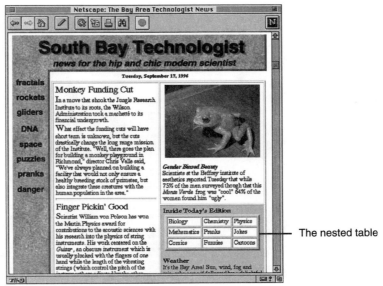

The nested table

The nested table tag starts between the <TD> opening and </TD> closing
cell tags.

Coloring Individual Cells

Coloring cells is as easy as specifying a background color for an HTML document;
the tag is the same. If a table is nested within a cell, the nested table inherits the
color of the cell surrounding it. You can either change the color of the entire table
with a BGCOLOR attribute in the TABLE tag or you can specify a color on a cell-
by-cell basis, as seen in Figure 3.5.

```
<TABLE WIDTH=190 CELLPADDING="2" CELLSPACING="3" BORDER="3"
➥BGCOLOR="#FFFFFF">
<TR>
<TD WIDTH=60>Biology</TD>
<TD WIDTH=60>Chemistry</TD>
<TD WIDTH=60>Physics</TD>
</TR>
<TR>
<TD BGCOLOR="#DEDE9C">Mathematics</TD>
<TD BGCOLOR="#DEDE9C">Pranks</TD>
<TD BGCOLOR="#DEDE9C">Jokes</TD>
</TR>
```

FIG. 3.5
You can specify a
different color for
each cell in a table.

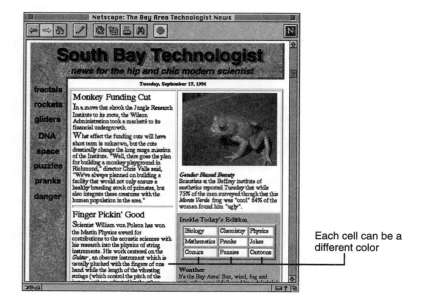

Each cell can be a
different color

The new table is specified white "#FFFFFF," so the first row of cells have a white background. The next three rows are each specified as a cream color.

Using a Transparent Image for Spacing

Tables can be difficult to position properly. After the masthead and sidebar were created and carefully fit, the table was added. However, the table looked a little too close to the sidebar. At that point we could start over and recreate these elements with a white border or we could use a *transparent image* to slide the table to the right slightly. The fact that GIF images can have a transparent color lets us accomplish this effect.

This process is covered in greater detail in Chapter 5, "Cool Effects with Images." Following are some quick steps that will create a transparent GIF image:

1. Open your paint program.

2. Create a square of any uniform color (255, 0, 0, for example).

3. Select that color and specify it as the image's transparency color.

   The transparency color must be the *exact* color of the image.

4. Scale the image so that it is small (one pixel in size is fine).

5. Save the image by using a name that you will recognize like "space.gif," "spacer.gif," or "trans.gif" (you have probably just created the image that you will use more than any other).

To use the transparent image just insert it by using the standard IMG SRC tag. Just scale the image to any size that you need; it is very easy to tweak the HEIGHT and WIDTH attributes to get the exact spacing that you want. You only need one completely transparent image for all of your applications. This spacer image is scaled to a very long, very thin image, as demonstrated in Figure 3.6.

FIG. 3.6
You don't see it, but the space a transparent image adds can be very helpful.

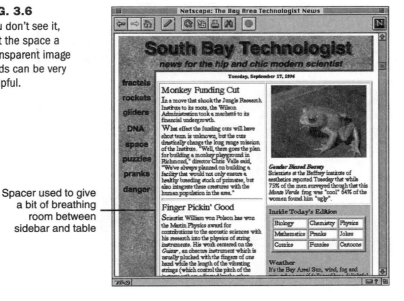

Spacer used to give a bit of breathing room between sidebar and table

```
<IMG SRC="pics/spacer.gif" HEIGHT=425 WIDTH=2 BORDER=0 ALIGN=LEFT
HSPACE=0>
```

N O T E Notice that BORDER=0. An invisible image with a border isn't very invisible. ▩

Being Aware of Critical Table Width

The right edge of the masthead must align with the right edge of the table, as seen in Figure 3.7. The sidebar image is 75 pixels wide. The table itself is 425 pixels wide. The image spacer you used is two pixels wide, meaning the total width of the masthead image should be 502 pixels wide. You have cut the masthead image to 508 pixels. These extra six pixels are from the cells' border being two pixels wide. Multiply two pixels by the number of cell borders (three), and the result is an additional six pixels.

FIG. 3.7
Here the right edge of the masthead and the table edge are perfectly aligned.

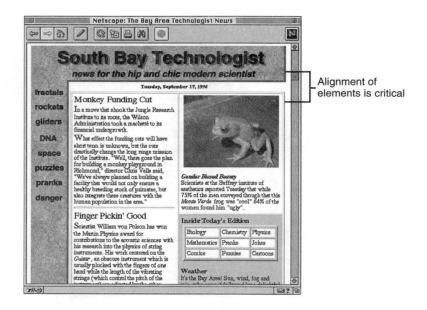

Alignment of elements is critical

  When making all of these adjustments make sure that you make a quick mock up where all of these factors come into play. Don't spend hours creating an intricate that is the wrong size by just five or six pixels.

Using Horizontal Rules as Dividers

You can create a separate cell for every horizontal line created. However, it is much easier to use the standard Horizontal Rule tag <HR>. Just make sure the

WIDTH and SIZE of the horizontal rule are set so that they match the overall look of the table cell borders.

The beauty of this approach is that your cells do not all have to be the same size. You can use the ROWSPAN attribute so that one cell can overlap as many adjacent cells as you like, and then use the HR tag to create the horizontal divisions.

```
<HR SIZE=4 WIDTH=200>
```

A size of "4" matches this page fairly well.

N O T E You can use images as HRs as well. This is an efficient use of graphic elements; the image is downloaded once then repeated for each occurrence.

Other Examples

Using Vertical Rules as Dividers

HTML does not provide a vertical rule, so make your own. You can insert an image as a vertical rule. Simply create a vertical graphic in your paint program, then add it in a cell.

Where Tables are Better than Image Maps

You are probably familiar with image maps; if they are new to you see Chapter 7, "Getting the Most From Clickable Image Maps." An image map is a graphical element that provides a graphical means for navigation. Of course, a carefully aligned group of images can provide the same function. Frequently, a table is used to aid in grouping these images. When making up your mind about which to use ask: "Am I going to change this map as I navigate from page to page?" If the answer is "no," use an image map. If the answer is "yes," then use a group of distinct images, as seen in Figure 3.8.

 T I P Using tables as navigational bars work OK as replacements for image maps in most cases. However, if you have irregular areas like what you find on road maps, or a scene full of objects, you're better off using an image map.

FIG. 3.8
This is a good prospect for using images within a table. Here, the image for the current topic is changed when it is on the topics page. This lets the user notice highlighting when a button is pressed.

Highlighted button indicates current location

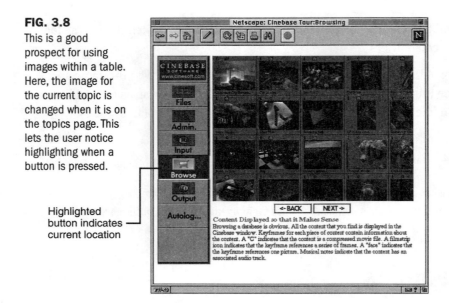

Trouble with Tables

Tables are very useful. However, they do present a series of challenges that you should be aware of. As a general warning, look at your table with several browsers and make sure that you can live with the results.

Tables Change Size

You can set table attributes in the TABLE tag and within each cell, however, that does not keep the cell from expanding if you cram too much text or too large of an image into it.

Fonts Add to the Problem

In addition to the table changing sizes without your permission, you also have to be aware that different browsers interpret text differently. For example, a line of text that you want to use as a heading with the setting FONT=4 may fit neatly into a cell when viewed with the Netscape browser on the Macintosh; however, when the same heading is viewed with a Netscape browser on a Windows 95 system, it may run over onto a second line. And, if explicitly setting font size doesn't work, then you surely cannot count on how a H1 or H2 tag will be interpreted.

Where to Go from Here?

- Chapter 4, "Using Frames Effectively"

  Many times people use tables when they should use frames and vice versa. Look at Chapter 4 to learn more about frames.

- Chapter 5, "Cool Effects with Images"

  Particularly useful if you found the transparent image example earlier in this chapter a little confusing.

- Chapter 7, "Getting the Most from Clickable Image Maps"

  Clickable image maps are powerful navigational tools. Don't get caught trying to make tables do everything when there are other powerful tools you can add to your Web pages.

## CHAPTER 4

Using Frames Effectively

Frames are one of the most powerful tags available in the HTML specification. They are great for organizing information, for providing navigational references and for opening new browsers automatically. The TABLES tag is commonly used when implementing features that frames do best. This chapter will focus on such things.

If frames are so easy to use and so powerful, why has it taken so long for people to start using them? Early browsers actually made frames a liability for browsing for two reasons:

When to use frames

Should you use frames or tables? Each has its place. Find out where frames can be indispensable.

How to organize frames

When you decide to use frames, the number of documents referenced at your site grows rapidly. Find out how to stay organized while using frames.

About nested frames

Frames can be nested. This feature makes creating complex sites much easier to deal with.

Borders and the borderless

How to control frame borders. You can also create frames without borders. This can make your layout look less "busy" and maintain the power of a frame layout.

Graphic problems

Aligning graphics as buttons can be kind of tricky. Here are a few tricks to save you some frustration.

Tricks for navigation

Using frames for navigation can be easy or complex. Following a few simple hints will guarantee implementing frames properly.

■ Some browsers did not (and still do not) support frames.

The Web master was obligated to provide two versions of the web site, one with frames, and one without. So implementing frames as only a "fancy option" looked like a burden rather than a liberating technology. This problem will go away as frames become a universally accepted tag.

■ Early browsers poorly implemented frames capabilities.

Frames were so poorly implemented that navigating a frames-based site was a very painful experience. For example, clicking the back button would not take you back to your last frame, rather it would take you to the last URL that you had visited. This led to a special navigational protocol when using a frame-based site; there was actually a "back in frame" option available. This problem has been resolved. Navigating frames is now as easy as any HTML document. ■

When Should You Use Frames?

Use frames anytime that you need a method for organizing information. Frames are particularly useful when you need one or more navigation bars available. Frames let you place a series of icons or hyperlinked text in an area that will always be available to the user. Unlike tables, you can "freeze" your navigational frames so that they never leave the visible page. When designed intelligently, you can change certain navigational areas and leave others static, as shown in Figure 4.1.

Use frames anytime you want to provide the user with step-by-step instructions on part of the page and a form to fill out on another. This way you can build in context-sensitive help for your users. This is a largely neglected application for frames. You have a customer who needs to fill out a technical support form, why not provide a resizable frame with instructions in it that the user can ignore or read carefully (see Figure 4.2).

FIG. 4.1

The top three navigational frames on the left change; the bottom frame changes depending on which section of the site you are browsing.

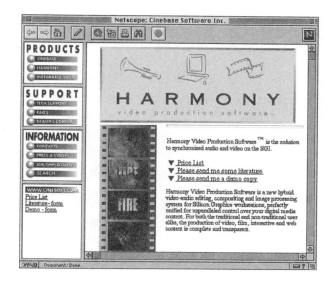

FIG. 4.2

Here, hints for filling out a complicated technical support form are included with the form.

Resizable frame with instructions

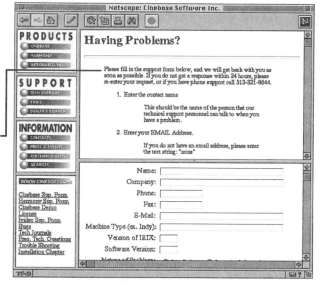

Avoid frames if you know that many people visiting your site will be using old-technology browsers. Or, if your site is simple enough that navigation is not an issue, you may want to keep your life simple.

How to Organize Frames

Sites that use frames are normally more complex than sites that do not. It is simply a matter of having several index files and HTML documents for each page that you create. For example, a traditional site that does not use frames and has 20 pages may be made up of only the 20 pages. It is easily possible for a frame-based site to reference 10 HTML documents per page with possibly 20 images as buttons. For example, Figure 4.2 shows a fairly simple frame-based site that uses six HTML documents to make up this one page, and 11 buttons are used as navigational devices. In addition, another 10 text hyperlinks are provided.

Sketch Your Site

When deciding how to organize your frames, it is worth taking a minute and drawing a quick sketch detailing the basic frame layout. This will give you a general idea of how to approach its construction. How many images will you need? What are the approximate sizes of different frames? How does each frame relate to each other? Many of these issues will come up as you continue with your plan, considering them now will save you a lot of time later. For example, the page in Figure 4.3 has some general index buttons across the top, a region of advertising along the right edge, a list of composers, and a "main-information frame." Without a quick sketch to start with, it would be difficult to guess what the general sizes of these regions should be. Trying to imagine what 100 pixels or 125 pixels really look like can be difficult. Getting the general ratios correct is easier with a sketch.

Develop Good Directory Structure and Naming Conventions

You build two types of HTML files when constructing frame-based sites. The first type of HTML file is the one that actually creates the columns and rows that make up your page with the FRAMESET command. You will probably have many of these "index files." Choose a name for these files so that they stand out; name them index_*filename*.html or *filename*_NX.html. You want to be able to find them quickly. Good names for these files are "index_navbar.html," and "classical_index.html." Use a naming convention that makes sense to you.

Create a separate directory for your graphics. Depending on how complex your site is you may want to create a directory for each major section, like a "techsupport" directory and a "marketing" directory. Changing names and directory structures halfway through a project can cause severe headaches. A good plan saves time and hassle.

Nesting Frames

Frames can be nested. That is, one FRAMESET tag can call another HTML document that contains additional FRAMESET tags. The first big question facing you when creating a frame-based site is how your frames should be organized. Should there be one index file with a host of FRAMESET tags in it or should you have a bunch of nested frames. Figure 4.3 shows four frames nested one inside of the other.

FIG. 4.3
Deeply nested frames look no different from a frame set established in one index file.

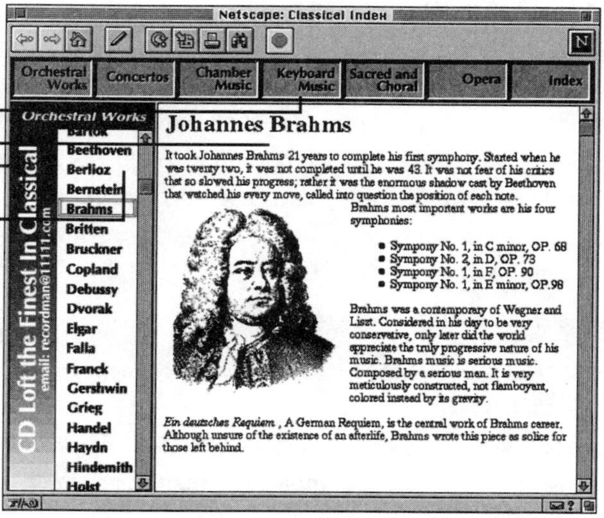

Four nested frames —

Advantages of a Single Index File

The advantage of having one file with all of your frameset commands in it is that you can change all of the windows in the frameset by modifying this one file. If you name each of your frames you still have the advantage of targeting any HTML document that you like to any window. In the following code you can see a frameset established in one index file. If these files get any more complex, it gets very difficult to understand how the frames are being established.

```
<FRAMESET ROWS="100%">
    <FRAMESET COLS="125, *">
        <FRAMESET ROWS = "93, 93, 113, *">
            <FRAME NAME="one" SRC="toc1.html" NORESIZE MARGINWIDTH="5"
➥MARGINHEIGHT="5" SCROLLING="no">
            <FRAME NAME="two" SRC="toc2.html" NORESIZE MARGINWIDTH="5"
➥MARGINHEIGHT="5" SCROLLING="no">
            <FRAME NAME="three" SRC="toc3.html" NORESIZE
➥MARGINWIDTH="5" MARGINHEIGHT="5" SCROLLING="no">
            <FRAME NAME="four" SRC="toc_sup.html" NORESIZE
➥MARGINWIDTH="5" MARGINHEIGHT="5" SCROLLING="no">
        </FRAMESET>
    <FRAME NAME="main" SRC="split.html">
    </FRAMESET>
</FRAMESET>
```

Advantages of Nesting Frames

Building a complex series of FRAMESET tags can be very confusing. It is actually easier to build a site with one nested frameset inside of another. That way you can add a frame, look at it, test it, modify it, then move to the next frame. It is really a question of how you want to replace certain elements as the user is navigating your site. For maximum flexibility and ease of construction a series of nested frames may be your best choice. The following code shows just how simple a frameset command can be.

```
<FRAMESET BORDER=1 ROWS="45,*">
    <FRAME NAME="navbar" SRC="classnavbar.html">
    <FRAME NAME="bottom" SRC="classbotindex.html">
</FRAMESET>
```

By nesting frames you can keep things very simple. This entire exercise was created with a set of files no more complicated than this. The first frame is the name of an HTML file that contains information (text and graphics). The second frame tag specifies the name of another index file which, like this file, points to one HTML file and another index file.

N O T E There is one disadvantage in using nested frames. To modify the appearance of your page significantly, you must open up a series of files to make the changes. ■

Construction Recommendations

When working with frames you are better off "roughing in" a Web site rather than trying to get it perfect the first time. One of the most important things to remember is that things can get very complicated in a hurry. Make sure that your basic frame structures are sound first. Then add finished graphics, links, and frame names. Construction tips and techniques are explained in the following sections.

Create a Temporary HTML File

Before creating final HTML files and carefully putting content in them, it is a good idea to construct your frame-based site by referencing just one empty temporary HTML file. An example of this file can be seen in the following code. Name it something like "temp.html." Then, reference this file instead of the final HTML file. This file will load instantly, and you won't get a series of error messages from your browser everytime you try to preview the basic table structure.

```
<HTML>
<HEAD>
<TITLE>Temp HTML</TITLE>
</HEAD>
<BODY BGCOLOR="#FFFFFF">
</BODY>
</HTML>
```

This simple HTML file is very useful for testing general layout.

Work with Borders On

In the next section, we discuss creating borderless frames. At this point, you are better off to work with at least a one-pixel border (see Figure 4.4). If you have the border set to "0" at this point you will not see the frames at all; they will be invisible. Once you are sure the frames are set up properly, then you can simply change the "1" to a "0" and the frame's borders will disappear.

Part
II

Ch
4

FIG. 4.4
You get a good idea
of what your page will
look like early on by
working with
BORDER=1.

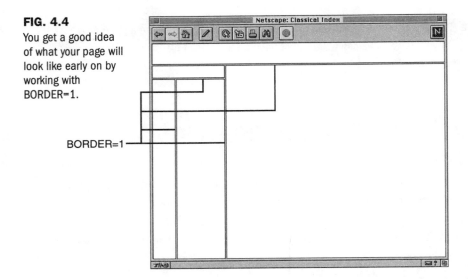

BORDER=1

Use Temporary Images

Don't bother creating and sizing your final buttons and graphics until you know
exactly how big you will need them to be. Instead, use a temporary image. Anything bright works. A single red or yellow square can be resized with the HEIGHT
and WIDTH image attributes to fit all areas where you want buttons and images to
fit. In Figure 4.5, you can see that an image with the word "TEST" painted on it is
used for this purpose.

Don't Add Links Right Away

HTML coding can get pretty ugly in a hurry (just take a look at the HTML in the
following code). Use as few commands as possible in your first pass. Later, adding
links and naming the windows becomes as easy as cutting and pasting text strings.
Keep things as simple as possible until everything looks good.

```
<BODY BGCOLOR="#313131"><NOBR><A HREF="orchindex.html"
TARGET="left"><IMG SRC="pics/orchwrks.gif" HEIGHT=38 WIDTH=80 BOR-
DER=0></A><A HREF="concertosindex.html" TARGET="left"><IMG SRC="pics/
concertos.gif" HEIGHT=38 WIDTH=80 BORDER=0><A
HREF="chamberindex.html" TARGET="left"><IMG SRC="pics/chamber.gif"
HEIGHT=38 WIDTH=80 BORDER=0><A HREF="keyboardindex.html"
TARGET="left"><IMG SRC="pics/keyboard.gif" HEIGHT=38 WIDTH=80
```

```
BORDER=0><A HREF="sacredindex.html" TARGET="left"><IMG SRC="pics/
sacred.gif" HEIGHT=38 WIDTH=80 BORDER=0><A HREF="operaindex.html"
TARGET="bottom"><IMG SRC="pics/opera.gif" HEIGHT=38 WIDTH=80
BORDER=0><A HREF="index.html" TARGET="_top"><IMG SRC="pics/index.gif"
HEIGHT=38 WIDTH=80 BORDER=0></NOBR></BODY>
```

FIG. 4.5
Here a test graphic
is used to see how
everything fits
together.

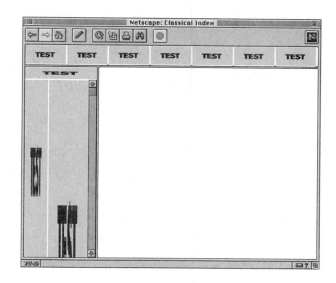

Don't start off with HTML that looks like this in the beginning. Adding all these
goodies is easy later.

Working with Frame Borders

You can now change the thickness and color of frame borders. This gives you
more control over the look of frame-based documents. In addition, you can make
them invisible and create seamless areas between graphics.

Controlling Border Color

Netscape Navigator lets you change border color. The command is
BORDERCOLOR="COLOR". The color value can be any of the accepted "color
names" or a Hex value to acheive any color that you like. This command can be
used in the FRAMESET tag or the FRAME tag.

```
<FRAME BORDERCOLOR="blue">
```

You can change border colors easily for the Netscape Navigator Browser. Use colors carefully, trying to match them with the rest of your look.

N O T E Each frame can only have a border of one color surrounding it. If two frames share a border, and if their border colors conflict, then the border color that was specified first in the HTML file is used. ■

Adjusting Border Width

The width of the borders can be adjusted to any pixel value that you like. Internet Explorer uses the FRAMESPACING attribute in the FRAMESET of FRAME tag.

```
<FRAMESET FRAMESPACING=2>
```

The preceding example sets the frame borders to two pixels wide.

Netscape Navigator uses the BORDER attribute in either the FRAMESET or FRAME tag to set the frame border width.

```
<FRAME BORDER=3>
```

The preceding example sets the frame borders to three pixels wide.

Although each browser usually supports the other tags as quickly as possible, it is not prudent to assume that these tags will work interchangeably. Since each browser ignores tags and attributes that it does not understand, the following works for both browsers:

```
<FRAMESET BORDER=1 FRAMESPACING=1>
```

The preceding example creates a one-pixel border in both Internet Explorer and Netscape Navigator.

 T I P Use frame borders for unique effects. Change the frame color to draw attention to a specific region (nothing like a red or yellow border to attract attention). Also use wide-frame borders to create "picture frame" effects. This is particularly useful if you're presenting artwork or photographs.

Borderless Frames

Creating borderless frames is pretty easy, but it does require some special care, particularly since Netscape Navigator and Microsoft's Internet Explorer have different methods of turning borders off. Figure 4.6 shows what a frame with a seamless border looks like.

FIG. 4.6
If you are careful, you can create seamless borders between frames.

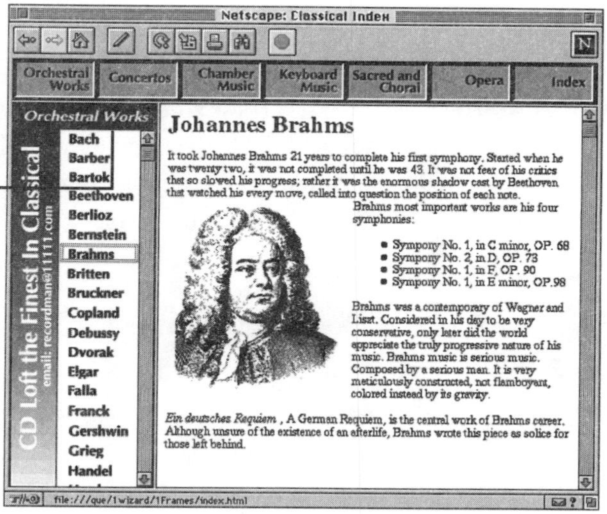

Seamless border —

Navigator uses FRAMEBORDER=NO while Explorer uses FRAMEBORDER=0 to turn frame borders off. In Navigator setting BORDER=0 implicitly turns FRAMEBORDER=NO, while in Explorer FRAMESPACING=0 should still be set if you want a seamless abutment of frames.

TIP Using the following line will create borderless frames in either browser.

```
<FRAMESET FRAMEBORDER=0 FRAMESPACING=0 BORDER=0>
```

The preceding example is the beginning of a FRAMESET command that will let you create borderless frames (of course, you need to add the desired ROWS and COLS attributes to build the frames).

Part
II

Ch
4

Problems with Graphics in Frames

Fitting graphics into frames can be tricky, particularly if your clients are using Netscape Navigator. Problems arise because the browser will not let you create a "marginless" frame where the graphic can fill the entire frame right up to the border. How to handle this problem is covered in the next section.

Dealing with HEIGHT and WIDTH Problems

When you specify a HEIGHT or WIDTH for your frame, Navigator does not create a frame with internal dimensions of that size; rather, some of those pixels are used in the construction of the borders and the margin. In addition, it does not let you set MARGINHEIGHT and MARGINWIDTH to "0" (see the previous section).

To solve this problem:

1. Get your borders set to the width that you want to use.

2. Create a stand-in of the graphic that you will create.

3. Adjust the FRAMESET HEIGHT and WIDTH parameters and the graphics HEIGHT and WIDTH parameters until you get a nice fit.

 Don't squeeze your graphics too tightly. You are better off to leave yourself a little room for error around the edges of graphics (particularly buttons). When you are creating these elements try to create a single color edge that will either blend into or contrast well with the background color. Then give yourself a few pixels to play with. As browsers change some of these settings may change.

Keeping Horizontal Graphical Elements Together

When you are creating a horizontal navigational bar made up of a series of separate buttons, instead of a long image map, you may find some of the buttons disappearing off the right edge of the screen if the browser's window is narrowed. This happens because the images try to break to the next line, and if you do not have NORESIZE and SCROLLING=NO set, you will get those nasty scroll bars appearing at the right edge of your navigational bar—not what you'd like to see. Figure 4.7 shows just such a problem; graphics "wrap around" and scroll bars are visible.

FIG. 4.7
You can get awkward results like this when the window is re-sized.

Graphics wrap to next line ⌐

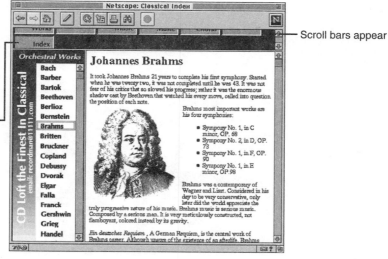

Scroll bars appear

To keep horizontal buttons together:

1. Set NORESIZE in the FRAME tag.

2. Set SCROLLING=NO in the FRAME tag.

3. In the HTML, surround the specified images with the <NOBR> </NOBR> tags.

The results of using the NOBR tag (as in the following HTML extract) can be seen in Figure 4.8, solving the problem originally encountered in Figure 4.7.

```
<BODY BGCOLOR="#313131">
<NOBR>
<IMG SRC="pics/orchwrks.gif">
<IMG SRC="pics/concertos.gif">
<IMG SRC="pics/chamber.gif">
</NOBR>
</BODY>
```

Part
II

Ch
4

CAUTION

In the preceding HTML sample, a series of three buttons are guaranteed to remain on the same line. Without including the NOBR tag you could end up with a situation like the one encountered in Figure 4.7.

FIG. 4.8
Now the buttons may extend beyond the screen border (just like an image map would). But they will not break to the next line, as they did in Figure 4.7.

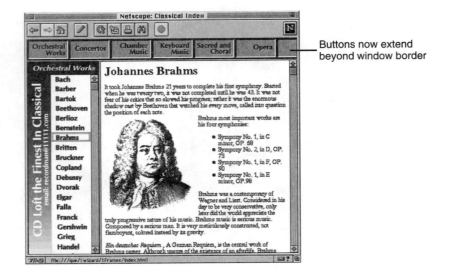

Buttons now extend beyond window border

Eliminating Space Between Buttons

Netscape Navigator leaves a space between buttons when you try to place them exactly next to each other (see Figure 4.9). This problem is easily solved. Following Figure 4.9 is the HTML that creates a problem for Navigator.

FIG. 4.9
Spacing between buttons when carriage returns are present.

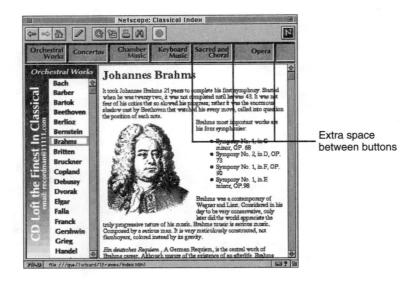

Extra space between buttons

```
<NOBR>
<IMG SRC="pics/orchwrks.gif" HEIGHT=38 WIDTH=80 BORDER=0>
<IMG SRC="pics/concertos.gif" HEIGHT=38 WIDTH=80 BORDER=0>
<IMG SRC="pics/chamber.gif" HEIGHT=38 WIDTH=80 BORDER=0>
<IMG SRC="pics/keyboard.gif" HEIGHT=38 WIDTH=80 BORDER=0>
<IMG SRC="pics/sacred.gif" HEIGHT=38 WIDTH=80 BORDER=0>
<IMG SRC="pics/opera.gif" HEIGHT=38 WIDTH=80 BORDER=0>
<IMG SRC="pics/index.gif" HEIGHT=38 WIDTH=80 BORDER=0>
</NOBR>
```

The carriage returns do not cause a problem for Explorer; however, they certainly do for Netscape Navigator. You can easily solve the problem so that the buttons look right in both browsers. Simply remove the carriage returns from the HTML file. Although less easy to read, this creates the effect we were looking for, as shown in Figure 4.10.

```
<NOBR><IMG SRC="pics/orchwrks.gif" HEIGHT=38 WIDTH=80 BORDER=0><IMG
SRC="pics/concertos.gif" HEIGHT=38 WIDTH=80 BORDER=0> <IMG SRC="pics/
chamber.gif" HEIGHT=38 WIDTH=80 BORDER=0> <IMG SRC="pics/
keyboard.gif" HEIGHT=38 WIDTH=80 BORDER=0><IMG SRC="pics/sacred.gif"
HEIGHT=38 WIDTH=80 BORDER=0><IMG SRC="pics/opera.gif" HEIGHT=38
WIDTH=80 BORDER=0><IMG SRC="pics/index.gif" HEIGHT=38 WIDTH=80
BORDER=0></NOBR>
```

Simply removing carriage returns lets the images touch each other.

FIG. 4.10
Spacing between buttons after the carriage returns are removed. You can compare this with Figure 4.9.

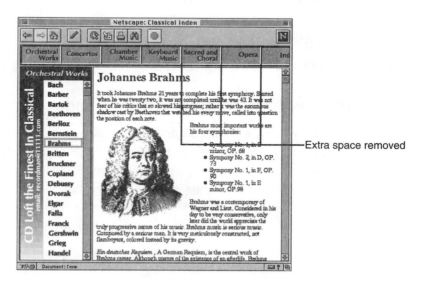

Part II

Ch 4

Navigational Tricks

Following are a few suggestions that may make life easier for you and your users. Remember, you implemented frames as a mechanism to make life easier for the people that visit your Web pages. Have you ever been to a Web site and gotten turned around, completely lost? Well, there's always that trusty "back button" at the top of the browser, but that is certainly a brute-force way to navigate. The following tips make quality assurance for frame development much easier.

Name All Windows

It is not necessary to name all windows when you are creating frames, however, naming each window lets you target exactly the subset of documents that you want to change. In this example (see Figure 4.10), clicking on the "Concertos" button only changes the list of composers in the "composers" window, while clicking on the "Opera" button changes the entire bottom portion of the browser by loading an "operaindex.html" index file in the "bottom" window. This is made possible by having named each window as they were constructed. One window was actually named "composers," so creating a link from a button and using the "composers" window as a target assures us where the specified HTML file appears.

```
<A HREF="concertosindex.html" TARGET="composers">

<A HREF="operaindex.html" TARGET="bottom">
```

Use Index Files to Redraw an Entire Window

The fact that you can only target one frame at a time can create some real problems. Now, most of these problems can be overcome in the planning stages by using nested frames and naming windows. However, if you paint yourself into a corner, don't worry about it. Just take the "top level" index file and rebuild it from there on down to get the layout that you want. This brute-force method is noticeable by the end user, but it's hardly an objectionable solution.

Here the Index button calls a file named "index.html", which is the start-up screen for this Web site. Notice how easy it is to change the look of a site in this manner.

You can use a relatively neutral look for the home page, a clean, conservative look for the Classical section and an avant-garde look for the Jazz section. For example, see Figure 4.11, which shows you a different layout.

FIG. 4.11
A whole new page layout by using an index file.

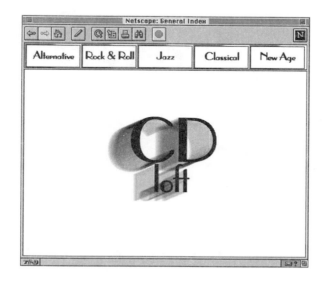

Part

II

Ch

4

Where to Go From Here?

■ Chapter 3, "Using Tables Effectively"

The functions of tables and frames are frequently confused. Check out the tables chapter for a clear comparison.

■ Chapter 7, "Getting the Most from Clickable Image Maps"

Use frames in ways that let you control what end users see. Chapter 7 shows a good example of combining frames and clickable image maps.

Sights

Cool Effects with Images

This chapter is all about graphic elements. Graphic formats have some limitations like color resolution and lack of true alpha channel. So, to get the best-looking pages, with minimal download time, understanding image formats and knowing a few tricks really helps. ■

Decide on the format

The two most popular formats, GIF and JPEG, should be used for different types of images.

Minimize image file size

By knowing what makes images large, you can work to keep them as small as possible and still get great-looking pages.

Create image effects

By using the LOWSRC tag you can create flashes and two-frame animations.

Add transparency to images

Since GIF lets you select a color as transparent, what are the advantages and limitations of this feature?

Be alert for new file formats

Progressive JPEG, PNG, and wavelets are all new formats. What promises do they hold? What features to they provide?

GIF or JPEG? That Is the Question

Currently, GIF and JPEG are the formats of choice for putting images on the Web. These two formats are like having two text formats available that are different but deliver the same results. These two formats have their own unique characteristics which make them particularly good for presenting different types of images. In general, GIFs are best for line art; JPEG is best for photographs and photo-realistic renderings, as shown in Figure 5.1.

FIG. 5.1
Use JPEG compression for photographs and GIF for line art.

If it wasn't for the slowness of the Internet, these formats wouldn't be important. Hi-resolution RGB or CMYK images without any compression would be available. However, since bandwidth is critical, compression is important. These formats provide compression in different ways and provide good-looking results with significant compression.

> **N O T E** PNG, a new format pronounced "ping," will replace GIF. For now, just think of PNG as GIF with more features. You can learn more about PNG later in this chapter. ■

When to Use GIF

Use GIFs on line art. Use GIFs when you have large regions of exactly the same color (these regions are much more likely to occur in drawings than photographs), as you see in Figure 5.2. Use GIFs when there are sharp boundaries between black and white.

FIG. 5.2
These images are good examples of GIFs. Notice the large regions of similar colors.

Same color, large regions

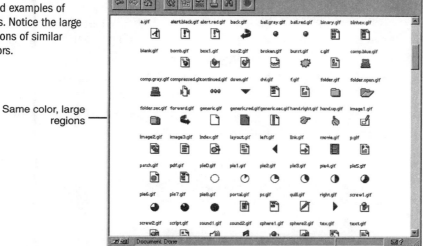

GIF also provides a few features that make it useful for particular effects, such as the following:

- GIFs let you choose a "transparency color" for the image. That is, any single color in the image can be selected as the transparent color, and every occurrence of that color in the image will be transparent.

- GIFs let you store more than one image in a GIF file. This lets you create very nice animations (see Chapter 8, "GIF Animations Are Fun and Easy").

- GIFs support "interlacing" so that images can appear to "fade in" instead of becoming visible one pixel at a time from the top of the image to the bottom.

CAUTION

GIFs can only contain 256 colors. If you have a full-color monitor, it is capable of displaying over 16 million colors. No matter what kind of tricks you try to play with compression or color optimization, you cannot cram 16 million colors into 256 colors elegantly.

When to Use JPEG

Use JPEGs for photographs and photo-realistic renderings, like the photograph in Figure 5.3. Any image that contains highlights and smooth shading and gradients works well as a JPEG. In addition, any image that looks bad as a GIF will probably look better as a JPEG; this is particularly true if you play with the JPEG's compression ratio; this variable compression ratio for JPEG makes it quite versatile. JPEG does not provide a transparency color, and for the types of images that JPEG usually is used for, selecting a single transparency color wouldn't be all that useful anyway.

FIG. 5.3

These images can be stored effectively as JPEGs. You can get compression ratios of 20:1 with good results.

Creating Transparent Images

If you have a GIF that has a large region of one color, you can make part of your image transparent. This is very helpful when you want to place your image over a background. Using transparency, the background will show through the transparent region, letting you get away from having each graphical element appear in the shape of a rectangle. GIF supports a single color that can be used as a transparent color, as shown in the dialog box of Figure 5.4. Once a transparency color is selected, this image can be placed over a textured background image, as in Figure 5.5, and the entire background color is transparent, only the text is visible.

FIG. 5.4
You can set the transparency value equal to the background color.

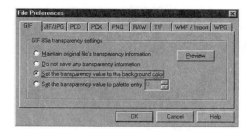

> **CAUTION**
>
> Only pixels that are exactly the transparency color will be transparent. Also, remember that all pixels in the image of the transparency color will be transparent. This does not work like an area fill where only contiguous pixels are affected. In addition, many graphics applications let you anti-alias graphics and text; this lets you smooth the text edges over the background to create very professional-looking effects. Anti-aliasing can be effective over a background. However, if you change the background color or use a pattern on the background, you can get very ugly results. This topic is covered in more detail in Chapter 6, "Time for a Background Check."

Part

III

Ch

5

FIG. 5.5
Once a transparency
color has been
selected the image
composites nicely
over a tiled back-
ground.

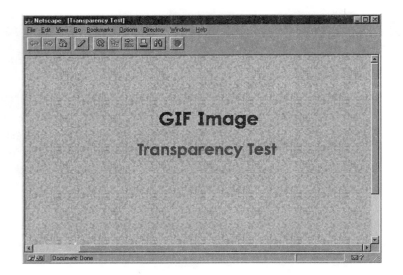

Achieving Better Transparency by Faking It

You can actually create better looking transparent images by not using transparency at all. Just make sure the image is created on a background that matches the background to be used in the HTML file. Of course, this is easiest to achieve when the background used in the browser is a solid color, and you know exactly what the background color will be. If applying the background images or colors is beyond your control, you should create transparent GIFs as described earlier.

How to Fake Transparency:

1. Find the image that you want to place over the background. Figure 5.6 is a painting of a ghost over a yellowed background.

2. Crop the image so you can see only the region that you want to use.

3. Use your paint programs to paint out the entire area that you do not want to appear in the browser (see Figure 5.7).

   Make sure you use the exact color of the background being used. Blend, feather, smudge, or paint the edges of the image to perfectly match the background. The results are visible in Figure 5.8.

FIG. 5.6
An image with a yellowed background. Even though the background is not extremely dark, it will show up as a "box" when inserted into an HTML document.

FIG. 5.7
Here the yellowish background of the image has been painted white. The image has been zoomed in so that good blending can be achieved between the white background and the edges of the ghost.

Part

III

Ch

5

CAUTION

This method produces great-looking results. However, if the background changes in the future, you will have to modify the image to fit the new background.

FIG. 5.8
The ghost on the left looks like it has a transparent background and is floating merrily in the air. The ghost on the right appears on its original background.

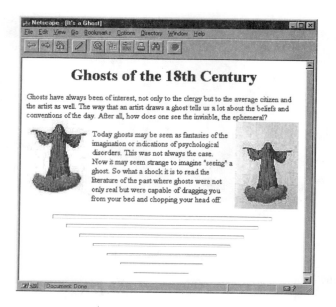

Casting Drop Shadows

Drop shadows help "connect" your graphic elements to the page. A drop shadow can very subtly make graphics look richer and more three dimensional or can be used to make graphics float over the page.

Casting Drop Shadows with Text

Drop shadows are most effective (and easiest to achieve) when you use them over a solid color background. Placing text, even nice-looking text, on a page can leave the page looking "flat" and uninteresting. Drop shadows help to create a 3D connection between the text and the page. The text is no longer just a word, but rather, a true graphical element that adds much visual complexity, interest, and texture to what you have to say.

To create a drop shadow:

1. Open a window in your graphics application that is exactly the same color of the background color in your HTML page.

It is a good idea to make sure this window is larger than what the final image will be. If you want to blur the drop shadow or offset the foreground text by a large amount, you do not want to run out of room. You can always crop this image later.

2. Choose the color that you want to use as the drop shadow.

   A medium gray almost always works great.

3. Type the line of text that you want, and apply it to the page.

   Remember, this text is the drop shadow, so you may want to offset it from the center of the window.

4. Now blur the image.

   This step is not necessary but will create a much more believable shadow.

 TIP If your application program has a motion-blur function, you might want to try it here. The results are usually much more interesting than just a standard pixel blur.

5. Type the foreground text and apply it to the window.

See Figure 5.9 for an overview of this process.

CAUTION

Blurring images will increase their size significantly if you are saving them as GIFs. As usual the question is: Will the effect be worth the extra download time?

FIG. 5.9
First the shadow is created, then blurred, then the text is applied over the shadow.

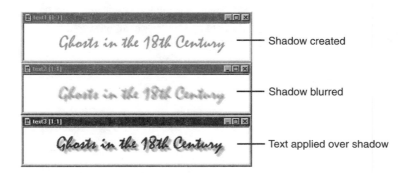

Float Graphics Off Your Page with Drop Shadows

You can make it look like any graphic is floating off your page. The process is quite similar to the one followed for text in the previous section. Figure 5.10 gives a quick overview of this process.

How to cast a shadow from a graphic:

1. Make sure your graphic's "background" is of one color and matches the background color of your HTML page.
2. Make a copy of your graphic, and convert it to a gray-scale image. This image will serve as the shadow.
3. Lighten this gray-scale shadow image if it is dark.
4. Blur the shadow image (again motion blur can do wonders).
5. Reopen your original image.
6. Convert it to a GIF if it is in a different format.
7. Select its background color as the transparency color.
8. Copy this image.
9. Paste it over the shadow image as a "transparent image."

See Figure 5.11 for the page that results.

 After this image is pasted over the background, there will probably be artifacts around its edges. Take the time to touch them up with your paint program.

Color ghost   Gray-scale ghost

FIG. 5.10

The original image is opened and converted to black and white. It is then blurred. The original image is opened again, and its background is selected as the "transparency color." This image is then cut and pasted over the shadow image. It is touched up to remove artifacts along its edges.

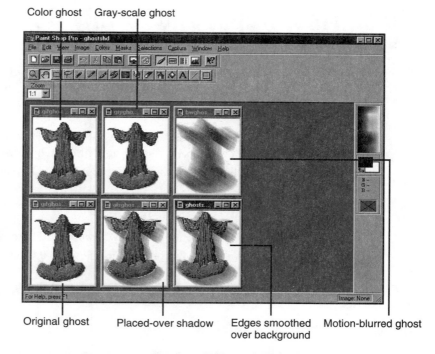

Original ghost   Placed-over shadow   Edges smoothed over background   Motion-blurred ghost

FIG. 5.11

When the graphic and text are placed on the page with drop shadows it looks like all the text on the page is floating. The fact that the ghost image has a large drop shadow, and that it is positioned very close to the text, adds to this effect.

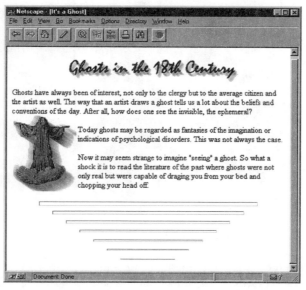

Part
III

Ch

5

Tricks, Tips, Traps, and Totally Cool Things

For real animations you will want to use GIF animations, as described in Chapter 8, "Gif Animations Are Fun and Easy," or use a multimedia application like Shockwave. However, there is an image extension that lets you create a quick two-frame animation. It is the LOWSRC attribute in the image tag.

So, if you want a lightning bolt to appear before our ghost fades in, you can create two images, as shown in Figure 5.12. Assuming that the Ghost image is named "ghost.gif" and the lightning bolt is named "light.gif," the HTML source should look like this:

```
<IMG SRC="ghost.gif" LOWSRC="light.gif">
```

Now, "light.gif" is a GIF file made up of only two colors and takes up almost no space at all. This image will flash on the screen followed by the ghost appearing.

FIG. 5.12
Use the lightning bolt with the LOWSRC attribute in the IMG tag. It will appear before the ghost appears.

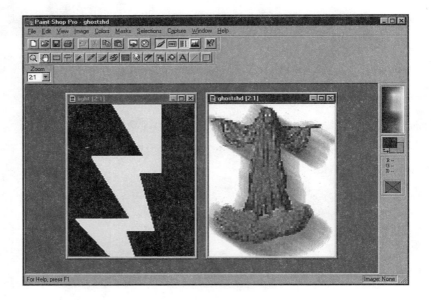

The Real Purpose for LOWSRC

Anytime you have an image that takes up a lot of memory you may want to consider using the LOWSRC attribute. This attribute was introduced so that you could put a quick representation of the final image on the screen, allowing your clients to get an idea of what was going on, and then slowly load the rest of the image as downloading permitted.

By using the HEIGHT and WIDTH image attributes you can use a very small LOWSRC image and blow it up to the size of the final image. This means very short download times for the LOWSRC image. Make sure the LOWSRC image still looks OK when you resize it. You can use the LOWSRC attribute as:

```
<IMG SRC="final.gif" LOWSRC="temp.gif" HEIGHT=120 WIDTH=160>
```

CAUTION

If you are going to use the LOWSRC attribute, make sure it is a very small image. Any information that is downloaded for the LOWSRC image is wasted when the final image downloads. You may find Interlaced GIF and Progressive JPEG better solutions to the download problem than using LOWSRC images.

Use Interlaced GIFs

Whenever possible save GIFs as "interlaced GIFs." They do not take up any more space than normal GIFs. Interlaced GIFs have the advantage of looking like they are "fading in" as they download. In most cases, viewers get a very clear impression of what the final image will look like when the GIF is only 25% downloaded.

Use Progressive JPEG

Progressive JPEG works much like interlaced GIFs; that is, the image gradually appears over time. Progressive JPEG files are generally slightly smaller than regular JPEGs and result in exactly the same final image.

Part
III

Ch
5

CAUTION

Although Netscape Navigator 3.0 and Internet Explorer 3.0 provide support for Progressive JPEG, not all browsers support this format. As always, know your audience.

Link to Hi-Res Images

If you want to provide high-resolution graphics to end users, but do not want your images to take forever to download, use a low resolution, highly optimized image, as a link to a different page with the high resolution graphics. The nice thing about this practice is that the "casual" viewer gets fast service, and the serious viewer can receive very large, high-quality graphics. You can also provide links to graphics that browsers do not typically support. For example, show a JPEG-compressed image of a landscape, then include a link to a PCD (a format used for PhotoCD's)version of the image.

Squeeze Those Images

Both JPEG and GIF provide controls for reducing the size and quality of images. Have you ever waited and waited for an image to download only to find out that it was not particularly interesting? Don't make your users wait forever. You can provide all the graphic punch that your audience can stomach while keeping download times reasonable. All you need to do is understand the image formats and how to compress them as efficiently as possible. Following are some very specific hints.

Hints for GIFs

Remember, GIFs are best used for images with large regions of the same color, like text on a solid background. Even if these images are large in size, they will compress nicely if they fit into this general "line art" type of graphic.

With GIFs you can reduce the size of the images by reducing the color palette. Some hints for effectively doing this include: do not "dither" GIFs, and do not anti-alias GIFs. Now those are two suggestions you will not be able to always pay attention to. As soon as someone tells you that your graphics look "jagged," you'll probably throw these optimizations out of the window.

Many graphics programs let you reduce the color palette for your GIFs. Reduce the color palette as much as possible. You can view the changes as you reduce them, so deciding on a cutoff point is subjective but relatively interactive (see Figure 5.13).

FIG. 5.13
When saving images in the GIF format, choose the lowest color resolution that will still give you acceptable-looking results.

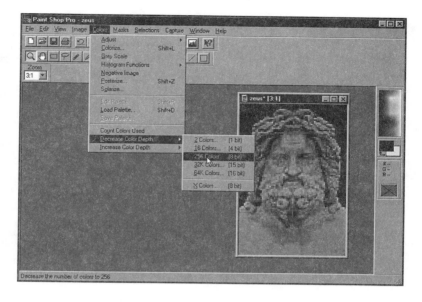

If you are using GIFs for text, consider replacing them with text. You can now specify particular type faces and colors. In many cases text works great.

Hints for JPEGs

Only use graphics that are photo-realistic in nature for JPEG compression. Having the correct image content to start off with is more than half the battle. If the image looks more like line-art, use the GIF format discussed previously.

The only way to compress JPEGs is to, well, compress them some more. When you save JPEGs you are given control over how much they are compressed. The more they are compressed, the poorer their image quality. The good news is that for photographic type images compression of 10:1 and even 20:1 still looks good. Depending on the application, the quality of JPEG images can be represented in different ways, such as a "quality factor" or a "compression ratio." As always, let your eyes be your guide.

Part
III

Ch
5

Be Ready for New File Formats

Things on the Internet are always improving (at least it's someone's idea of improving). Image formats have been relatively stable with two complementary and versatile formats like GIF and JPEG. However, for legal reasons and others, new image formats are on their way. Two such formats include PNG and Wavelets as discussed in the following sections.

PNG—The Next Great Format?

GIF has been a great format. But, it has some obvious limitations. For example, it does not support 24-bit or 32-bit color. That one color transparency limitation is kind of a joke, instead of having a true eight-bit alpha channel available. Standards for a new GIF were already in the works when in 1987 UNISYS (the company that developed GIF for Compuserve) decided to enforce its patent on the LZW compression and decompression algorithms. Well, that was the final straw, so a new, improved version of GIF was developed, and it was named PNG (pronounced "ping").

PNG will provide all the features of GIF, plus better transparency and the ability to provide true lossless compression. However, since PNG lets you store and transmit 32-bit images, it is very easy to create very, very large files. Features like animation and interlacing are being maintained, and it is possible to get a good idea of what the final image will look like much sooner than with interlaced GIF images.

Many graphics packages already support PNG. Most browsers should support PNG shortly. If you would like to start creating and distributing PNGS today, there are already plug-ins that you can obtain for your browser.

Wavelets

Just as PNG is the challenger for the GIF throne, Wavelets will challenge JPEGs for the image types that JPEG is now particularly good at representing.

Both JPEG images and Wavelets look "good" at similar compression ratios. However, Wavelets are less blocky looking than JPEGs. Wavelet's artifacts are more organic looking.

Wavelets do have some additional features:

- Wavelets allow "focusing."

  This feature allows user-selected image regions to maintain higher visual detail during compression. That is, you can choose the region that will suffer the most during compression, then compress the rest of the image like crazy, ending up with a good-looking, very small image.

- Wavelets allow progressive downloading.

  Progressive downloading allows part of the image to be viewed as it is downloaded. As additional image data is downloaded it "fills in" regions that appear blurry. The best feature of progressive downloading is that overall, it doesn't take any longer than downloading the entire image in an uncompressed format. In this respect Wavelets and Progressive JPEG are similar.

- Wavelets allow "magnification."

  With intelligent implementation you can provide different resolutions of the same image. When a higher resolution is downloaded by the user it uses the information in the low-resolution version as a starting point and downloads all new image data.

Will Wavelets replace JPEG? Certainly not immediately. Again, browser support is critical for Wavelets success. There are currently plug-ins available. You should check them out. This is very promising technology.

Part
III

Ch

5

Where to Go From Here?

- Chapter 8, "GIF Animations Are Fun and Easy"

  You can use that handy, old GIF format for doing some pretty cool animations. Check out this chapter.

Time for a Background Check

Making good use of backgrounds can add that something special to your Web pages. Making poor use of backgrounds will make your Web pages look amateurish or even illegible. ■

Create seamless tiles from your own images

You can create your own background images; removing the annoying seam is the trick.

Cast a shadow on your background

It's easy to make it look like foreground elements are actually casting shadows on your background.

Create a "shelf" along the left edge of your pages

With a very small image you can create a nice border along the left edge of your pages.

Use solid colors as backgrounds

Why do you see so many black and so many white backgrounds on the Web? They're automatic. They take almost no download time, and with a tag like <BODY BGCOLOR=#FFFFFF> you can add a white background.

Scrounge Around for Your Backgrounds

Fire up your favorite search engine. Type in the words "tiled backgrounds." Sit back and relax as almost every type of background that you'd ever care about is made available to you. Almost all backgrounds are free. Netscape has a background library that you can link to. There is also a great background library called the "KPT Background Archive." Even if you have your heart set on creating your own backgrounds, these resources will provide inspiration and raw material that you can modify.

NOTE If backgrounds become your life, you should check out Kai's Power Textures and Terrazzo. These products let you make the geometric and algorithmic patterns that are very intriguing. ▪

Seams Are Seemly—Creating Seamless Background Tiles

Most images can be modified to be used as backgrounds. In this exercise you will see a rather unlikely image turned into a rather nice background. Hey, if you can make a background out of a frog sitting on a leaf, almost anything will work. See Figure 6.1.

When you try to use any image as a background, you will almost certainly have very noticeable seams. This is true even in a case when the overall image is fairly uniform in color. Create an HTML file that includes the background image, then open it with your browser. This is a good first step to see how much work you have ahead of you. See Figure 6.2

Offsetting the Image

The first step in creating a seamless image is to create an "offset" of the original image. You can either perform this operation manually, or use a paint application that provides this feature automatically.

FIG. 6.1
This frog will become a background tile.

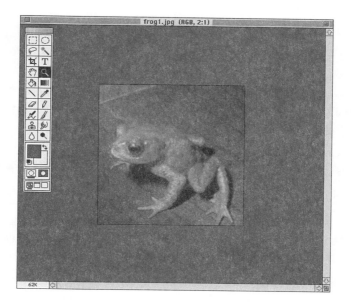

FIG. 6.2
A typical scene when you add an image as a background.

These seams
must go

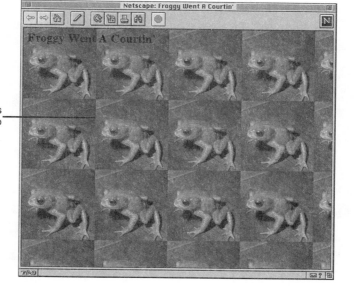

Part

III

Ch

6

To offset the image manually:

1. Arrange four copies of the original image in a two-by-two grid.

   Let's say this original image is 150 × 100 pixels in size. Their borders must be perfectly aligned with no white space between them. Do not overlap the images or this process will not work. The composite image, in this example, will measure 300 × 200 pixels.

2. Crop a region over the exact center of this composite image that is the exact size of the original image.

   In this case, the image that you crop will be a 150 × 100 pixel image cut from the center of the composite image.

This results in your new offset image. The seams of the original image should cut this offset image exactly in half horizontally and vertically.

Of course, an easier method for creating the offset image is to use a paint application that provides an offset command. In this case the offset feature of Adobe Photoshop is demonstrated in Figure 6.3.

FIG. 6.3
Make sure that Offset is set to exactly half of the image's size.

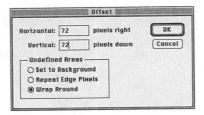

Just follow these steps to set Offset:

1. From the Filter menu select Other.

2. From the Other menu select Offset.

3. Enter an offset value that is exactly half of the original image's size.

   In this case you enter 72. Our original image was 144 × 144 pixels.

4. Make sure the Wrap Around button is selected. See Figure 6.3.

5. Click OK. See Figure 6.4 for the resulting image.

FIG. 6.4
The image is now offset. All those nasty seams are visible.

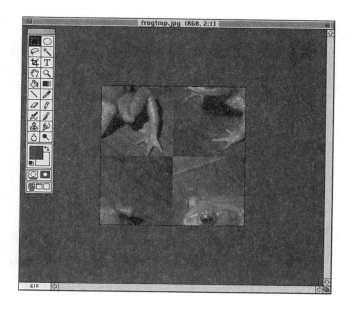

Now, if you are not too fussy about the way the seams are joined, you can just blur the edges and get an effect that is better than the original. See Figures 6.5 and 6.6.

FIG. 6.5
Use the smudge tool to blur the edges.

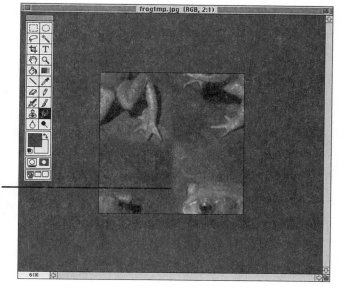

Edges are blurred ——— with the smudge tool

Part
III

Ch
6

FIG. 6.6
With blurred edges the image is only slightly improved.

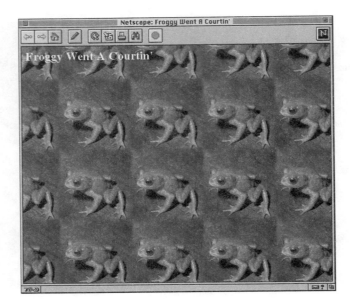

Smudging works OK. But with just a little bit more care you can greatly enhance the repeat-pattern nature of the image. Look for lines, or areas near the seams that are similar. Then the idea is to join these similar edges across the seams. In this case, you look for veins in the leaves that just happen to line up with each other. In places where they don't line up, you can carefully extend lines that begin on one side of the seam across the seam. See Figure 6.7.

It is this continuity across the seam that is more convincing to your eye than a smudged edge. If you look at many of the patterns used on the Web you will notice, if you magnify them many times, that the seams are still quite visible. However, the creator was careful to make sure that lines, patterns, and colors were clearly continuous across the seams. The final result in Figure 6.8 is not perfect, but certainly a good start.

N O T E If you don't want the frogs to extend off the screen, simply "offset" them again in your paint application and save the image. ■

FIG. 6.7
Here a vein is being extended across the leaf.

Extend lines across the seams of the image

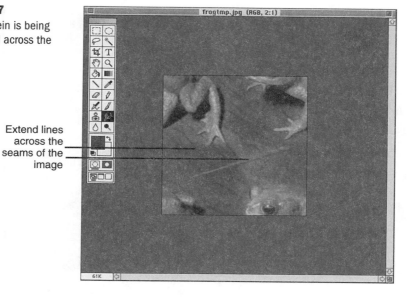

FIG. 6.8
Now the seams are gone, and you have a nice repeating tile that has some depth to it.

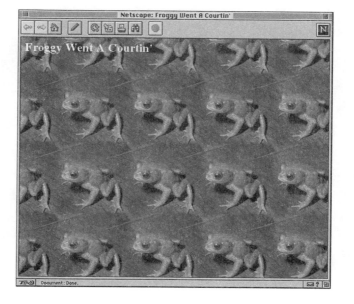

Part

III

Ch

6

Cast a Shadow on Your Background

Sometimes, you want to place graphics on your page, and you want to somehow connect them with your background. In a case like this it is best to use a background that works well if it does not line up perfectly with itself. That is, it shouldn't show noticeable seams most of the time. Figure 6.9 shows a background that is a marginally good choice.

FIG. 6.9
This background is pretty irregular and will work just fine. The more noticeable the exact patterns are in an image the harder they are to use for this application.

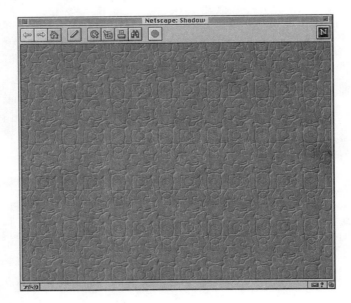

Create a Banner of Tiled Images

The first step is to create one large image made up of tiles. In this case the tile is 96 pixels in size. So you will copy, paste, and position five of the images in a row. This image will be saved and used as an image that you can then render text over. See Figure 6.10

You then render text over this composite image and insert it into the body of the document just like any image.

```
<BODY BACKGROUND="tiled_image_name.gif">
<IMG SRC="title_bar_name".gif ALIGN=LEFT BORDER=0>
```

When the image is placed in the window it fits right in. See Figure 6.11.

FIG. 6.10
The original tile is replicated and pasted together. The alignment is critical. You do not want to be one pixel off.

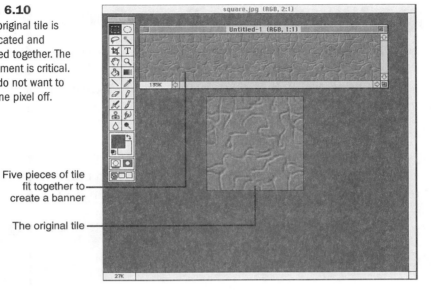

Five pieces of tile fit together to create a banner ——

The original tile ——

FIG. 6.11
This text is just floating over the background. Really?

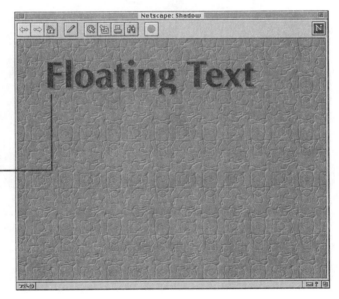

No visible seam where graphic meets background ——

Part

III

Ch

6

Creating a Nifty Shelf to Store Some Text

You've seen the ledges or shelves along the left edge of many Web pages. You should try them yourself. They are fun and easy to create and don't take a whole heck of a lot of time to download. They work just like the background images you've used before.

1. Create a long narrow image.

   In this case you create a GIF with a white background that is 800 pixels wide and 40 pixels high. That way it will extend well off the right edge of most browsers. You don't want this tile to visibly tile to the right. See Figure 6.12.

FIG. 6.12
An 800X40 pixel white image is the basis for our background.

800X40 pixel white image

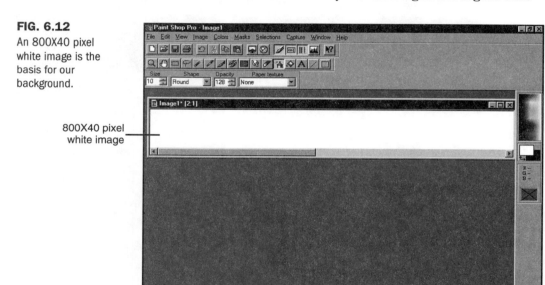

2. Now zoom in on the left edge of this image.

   You'll only be modifying the left 100 pixels, so get in close. You can create a smooth edge, something that looks like a bevel, an edge of a torn page, a spiral-bound notebook—you name it. Another nice trick is to fade the edge into the rest of the background color (in this case white) so you get a real 3D effect. See Figure 6.13 for the effect you have chosen.

FIG. 6.13
By making sure the top edge and the bottom edge lie exactly at the 100-pixel mark, it doesn't really matter what you do in between. You know the background will repeat seamlessly.

By starting and ending at the 100-pixel mark, you assure seamless tiling

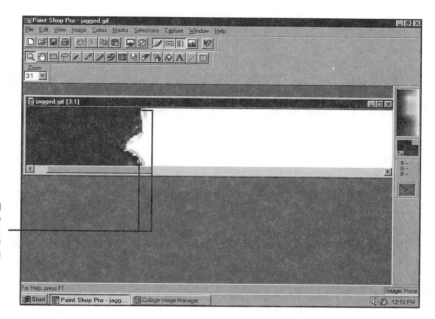

3. Save the image in the format of your choice.

In this case, there aren't many colors, and you have long continuous regions of white, so the GIF format works nicely. You get this entire background for less than 1K. See Figure 6.14.

FIG. 6.14
This is a nice effect and can be easily changed to add interest to your pages. It also does a nice job of showing the client that this region is set aside for a special purpose.

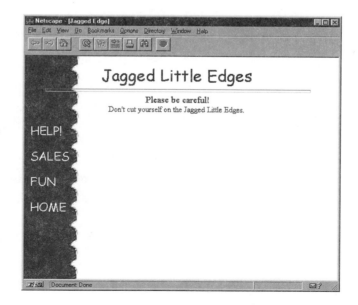

Part

III

Ch

6

Tips for Background Tiles

Following are a few tips for background images.

- Use gradients sparingly.

  Gradients really stretch the capability of your client's display. You will almost always get annoying banding when you stretch a gradient across the full screen.

- Use backgrounds with tables or frames.

  In the shelf example, you probably want to use a table or a frame to keep text from flowing over onto the shelf. See Chapters 3, "Using Tables Effectively," and 4,"Using Frames Effectively," for more information about exactly how to do this.

- Keep your backgrounds small.

  Want to really annoy someone? Make them wait a long time for your background image to download.

- Reuse backgrounds.

  Once the client's system has cached a copy of the background, you can use it practically for free. If you're careful and select good backgrounds, reuse them.

- Stay away from busy backgrounds.

  Hopefully, you are saying something worth reading on your Web pages. If that is the case, keep the contrast between the background and text high, so that people can read the text.

Use Solid Backgrounds

Solid backgrounds are the one sane element in what sometimes seems to be a rather insane medium. You should use solid backgrounds unless you have a particular reason for choosing a specific background graphic.

- Black backgrounds are great for placing computer-rendered objects over. Usually, these graphics anti-alias to black, so they fit on black pages seamlessly.
- White backgrounds make it easier to read darker colored text. In addition, if you create most of your graphics so that they fade to white, you'll be in great shape when you want to plop these elements on your page.
- Solid backgrounds require no download time.

Add a white background with this command line:

```
<BODY BGCOLOR="white">
```

There are only a few colors that you can specify by name. RED, GREEN, BLUE, BLACK, WHITE (there are others, but they are less standard).

However, you can specify any background color using hexadecimal numbers. For example:

```
<BODY BGCOLOR=#FF0000>
```

results in a red background color.

The hex scale has 16 possible digits per place, instead of the 10 possible values that base ten has. For specifying color values, each pair of hex numbers specifies a color in RGB color space, with the first two digits representing RED, the next two GREEN, and the final two BLUE.

Remember "0" is the lowest value you can assign; "F" is the greatest value; that leaves "8" halfway between 0 and F.

For example:

#888888 - represents 50% gray.

#000000 - is black

#FFFFFF - is white

If this stuff still doesn't make any sense to you, don't worry. Just get out your hex calculator, enter the value for a color channel, then hit the ->HEX button. There are also HEX calculators available on the Web. Good Luck!

Part

III

Ch

6

Where to Go from Here?

This chapter has been all about backgrounds. You can find information about backgrounds and images in a variety of places. In addition, there are a lot of good background libraries and archives out there for you to explore.

- Chapter 5, "Cool Effects with Images"
  A good reference for image formats and modifications that you can make to images.

- **http://home.netscape.com/assist/net_sites/bg/backgrounds.html**

  Netscape has a library of background images that you can browse through.

- **http://the-tech.mit.edu/KPT/bgs.html**

  You can also find oodles of backgrounds at this MIT KPT Background Archive.

Getting the Most from Clickable Image Maps

Clickable image maps let you define regions of an image, so that when you click over the region an action occurs (usually an HTML document opens). Clickable image maps are one of the most underused features of HTML. With the proper tools, they are easy to create, and fun to use. This is particularly true since you do not need a server to process your image maps anymore. All popular browsers support what is called "client-side image maps" (CSIM). ▪

What an image map is

An image map is really only a set of shapes and coordinates specified in a file that your server or browser understands.

When to use an image map

Image maps work well anytime you want an end user to click a specific region and load an HTML document. But they really come into their own when you want to define irregular and circular shaped regions.

The difference between server-side and client-side image maps

Don't use server-side image maps unless your boss makes you or offers you alot of money to do it!

How to build an image map

You need a picture, some basic HTML know-how, and an image map utility application to make things really easy.

The benefits and drawbacks of image maps

Although image maps can provide unique functionality, they are not the only solution for every graphic link.

What's an Image Map?

An image map is two things:

It is a picture.

It is a set of shapes and coordinates that define "hot areas."

As your cursor moves over the screen, and it passes through one of these hot areas, your arrow pointer turns into a selection pointer and the HTML document that you will jump to appears on the status line of your browser. By clicking over a hot area, you jump to the desired HTML document. See Figure 7.1.

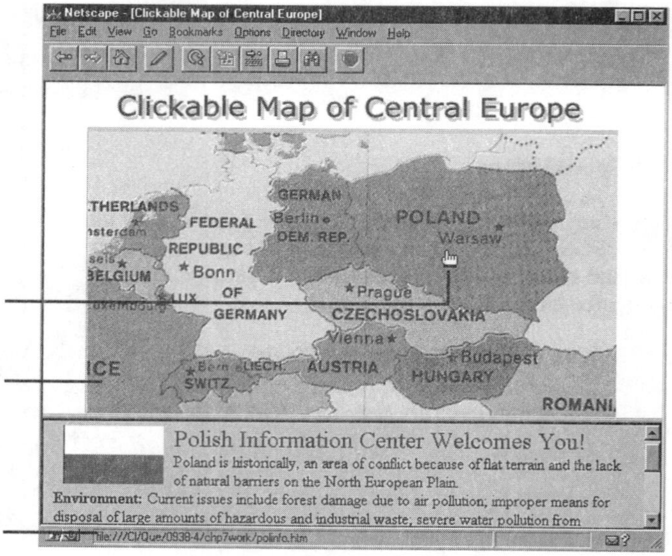

FIG. 7.1
This map includes intelligent use of frames (as discussed in Chapter 4, "Using Frames Effectively"). Click this out-dated map, and you get some information.

Selection pointer

Hot area

HTML address on status line

N O T E   The previous paragraph discusses the feedback that you get when using client-side image maps. Server-side image maps work somewhat differently and are discussed later. ■

When Should You Use an Image Map?

Many times image maps are used over a graphical "navigation bar." Image maps are easy to use in such situations, but they could just as easily be replaced by a series of individual images positioned carefully. And, although image maps are not impossible to modify, they can get confusing, especially if you've been away from them for a month or so. Figure 7.2 shows a very complex navigation bar that is made up of a series of images. This Web master believes individual graphics with direct links to other HTML documents are faster to modify than image maps.

FIG. 7.2
Is this navigation bar an image map or a series of individual images? Hint: it's not an image map.

Navigation Bar —

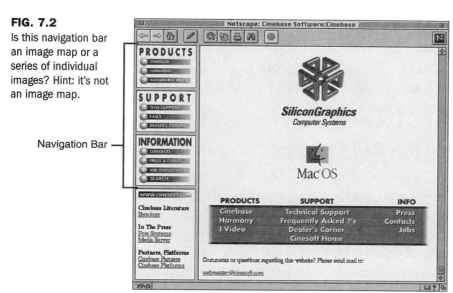

Image maps work best when you are trying to define irregular or circular regions. This is exactly where good old rectangular graphics are at their weakest. Image maps would work great for the following applications:

- You have an exploded view of a parts assembly and would like more information about the part, like its cost or inventor number, to appear when you click it.

Part
III

Ch
7

- You have a floor map of a building. When you click each room you would like some information about who works there to appear.

- You want to create a "virtual tour" of a museum. When someone clicks a painting or sculpture, you would like to present the viewer with a high-resolution version of the piece with some historical information (in some ways it's better than being there!).

- Image maps work very well for—of course—maps, world maps, county maps. See Figure 7.1 for an example.

It's Server Side versus Client Side

There are two types of image maps. One type requires access to and the functioning of a server. The other type runs locally on your computer, the functionality is built into your browser.

Server Side—The Bad Old Days

Originally, image maps required a special, image-map script to be running on the server. That's what was required to use image maps. With a server-side image map the mouse coordinates are tracked over the browser window. When the mouse is clicked the coordinates are passed to the server. The server then looks in the map file and finds the URL associated with the coordinates. This URL is then sent to the client. If this sounds complicated, it is, and it causes additional problems.

- You need access to a server.

- The server must be running an image map CGI script, or you must have access to the server's CGI-bin directory, so you can load your own image map CGI script.

- Communication with the server must be fast and reliable or the viewer could spend time waiting for the server to respond.

- You need to be connected to the server to test the operation of your map (this can be so bad at times that you may actually find yourself installing server software on your own PC just to relieve some of the hassle of uploading, and uploading, and uploading files to the server).

Client Side—The Only Way to Fly

Because of these drawbacks, browsers started supporting image maps internally (there went the really small browsers). Now the image map information is downloaded with the HTML document. This has some advantages.

- You don't need a server to build, test, or use your image maps.

- You don't need to mess with CGI scripts (not here anyway).

- Access to the image-map data is instantaneous.

- Your browser knows more about your map than it used to. Now, when you move the pointer over the browser window it can change states when it passes over a "hot" region. In addition, you can see the name of the URL that will be loaded when you click. If these URLs are intelligently named, you may be able to help your user decide where to click. Figure 5.3 shows the type of feedback that you can get from a client-side image map, where the pointer is on Poland and the information is displayed in the bottom frame.

N O T E You can support both server-side and client-side image maps in the same HTML file. Server-side image maps do have an advantage in that they will support very old browsers. Know your audience. You may not have to worry about server-side image maps at all. ■

FIG. 7.3
You can tell which regions are hot and which URL will be loaded when using a client-side image map.

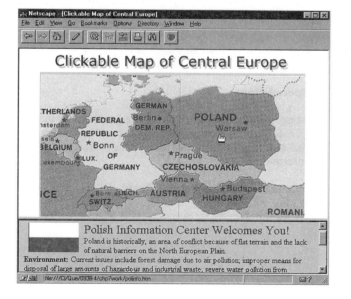

Part
III

Ch
7

Creating a Good Image Map

You can create image maps with a graphics application and a text editor. However, if you are defining complex regions, there are several good utility applications that you can use to greatly aid in your creation of image maps. On the Macintosh, WebMap is a good application. On Windows machines, Map This! and Map Edit are both good applications. These are all very limited in their use and therefore take almost no time to learn.

To create an image map:

1. Create an HTML file with the graphic that you want to use as the background image. Just use the <IMG SRC="mapname"> tag.

   ```
   <IMG SRC="cneurope.gif">
   ```

2. Open your map creation application. In this case, MapEdit.

   You may be prompted for whether you want to open a ".map" file for server-side image maps or an HTML document for client-side maps.

3. Choose the HTML document that you just created.

   You will be presented with a list of images as specified in the HTML document.

4. Select the image for which you want to create a map. See Figure 7.4.

FIG. 7.4
Use the dialog box to
open or create an
image map.

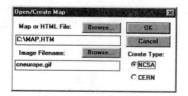

5. Select the HTML and the image that you want to create a map for.

6. Use the applications drawing tools to draw shapes over the image.

   In the case of Central Europe it's hard to imagine using a rectangle or a circle to define a region (it's not Colorado you know), so you'll be using polygons. See Figure 7.5.

 TIP How many polygon's are enough? Well, it's really up to you. Each time you click the mouse, two numbers will be added to your map file. But since these numbers are added and edited with this application program, make sure that you add enough to do a good job of representing the country's shape. On the other hand, remember if someone wants information about Poland, they are probably not going to see how close they can click to its borders, and no one will see your artwork so you don't have to be exact.

FIG. 7.5
Here, the outline of the former West Germany is being traced. Use enough points to represent its shape. For a shape like this, between 25 and 50 points will give you a good representation of this country's shape.

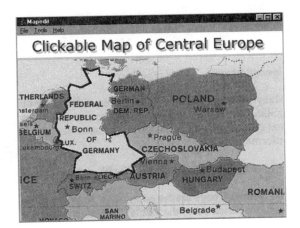

7. Once you have finished drawing the shape you can test it by clicking it.

8. You will now want to specify a URL for the HTML file that you want loaded when you click the region. See Figure 7.6.

FIG. 7.6
Click the region and specify a URL. The URL does not have to exist at this point. No checking occurs. Select a name that you plan on using.

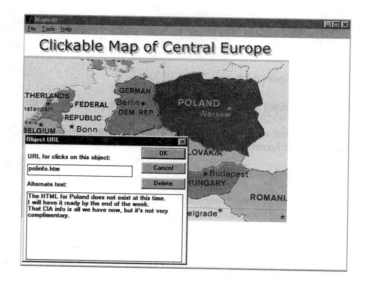

9. Draw each region and specify an HTML for it.

10. Save the file.

N O T E What about overlapping regions. Your browser processes regions from the top of the list to the bottom of the list. So, if any regions overlap, the region specified closest to the top of your HTML file will be processed. ◼

Making the Image Map Special

Now, it's time to look at the image map file. Understand how it is put together, and make a couple of modifications to it so that it works even better.

This is the HTML for the file; only East Germany, Switzerland and Poland have been specified at this point.

```
<HTML>
<HEAD>
<TITLE>"info"</TITLE>
</HEAD>
<BODY BGCOLOR="#FFFFFF">
<CENTER>
<IMG SRC="cneurope.gif" USEMAP="#cneurope">
</CENTER>
```

```
<MAP NAME="cneurope">
<AREA SHAPE="POLYGON"
coords="211,93,198,98,186,98,181,119,199,125,182,134,188,148,185,
➥154,178,167,164,173,166,184,162,196,186,207,209,204,215,208,278,
➥184,270,158,266,147,257,128,263,118,260,98,225,83"
HREF="egerinfo.htm">
<AREA SHAPE="POLYGON"
coords="355,74,326,78,310,82,303,89,262,100,263,115,258,131,269,140,
➥271,156,268,163,277,183,298,197,307,197,307,205,316,212,320,207,320,
➥202,337,213,356,220,369,232,377,228,384,238,402,234,415,235,422,232,
➥451,245,448,226,482,200,481,189,468,170,469,155,459,148,465,139,478,
➥136,466,92,454,84,447,87,381,83,377,87,358,87,352,73,352,73"
HREF="polinfo.htm">
<AREA SHAPE="POLYGON"
coords="132,276,130,280,96,287,77,313,77,321,87,313,96,330,116,328,
➥128,315,141,331,148,316,166,318,165,311,172,308,173,299,164,303,149,
➥293,156,286,150,280,135,281" HREF="swisinfo.htm">
<AREA SHAPE="default" NOREF>
</MAP>
</BODY>
</HTML>
```

Taking a Good Hard Look

Remember, we started out with only:

```
<IMG SRC="cneurope.gif">
```

Mapedit has modified this to read:

```
<IMG SRC="cneurope.gif" USEMAP="#cneurope">
```

Then, it has specified the map file as:

```
<MAP NAME="cneurope">
```

N O T E The MAP NAME can be any name that you like as long as it is referenced
properly by the USEMAP attribute in the IMG tag. ▨

Getting It Frame Ready

This map image fits into the top frame of a two-frame HTML document. See Chapter 5, "Cool Effects with Images," for more information about working with Frames. When the map is clicked we want to direct the specified URL to the bottom frame that contains information about the country we selected (this frame has been named "INFO" with the frameset command of the parent document).

Part

III

Ch

7

> **CAUTION**
>
> The changes you make from here on are not normally remembered by your map-editing applications. This means that before tweaking your HTML document for maximum performance you had better finish your map creation task.

To accomplish this we simply need to add the line TARGET="INFO" to the end of each HREF attribute. For example:

```
...156,286,150,280,135,281" HREF="swisinfo.htm" TARGET="INFO">
```

Now, when Switzerland is clicked, the HTML file named "swisinfo.htm" is loaded into the "INFO" window.

It's So Refined, It's Almost... European?

Just a couple more touches and we'll be ready for true international exposure.

You can see that the IMG tag does not have a BORDER attribute listed. On most browsers this means that we'll get a default border. So let's change:

```
<IMG SRC="cneurope.gif" USEMAP="#cneurope">
```

to:

```
<IMG SRC="cneurope.gif" BORDER=0 USEMAP="#cneurope">
```

And what happens when we click outside the mapped region, like in the middle of the ocean? Warn the user that he is about to make a mistake. Then, after he makes a mistake, tell him that he made a mistake.

The last line in the map file is:

```
<AREA SHAPE="default" NOREF>
```

This tells the browser which HTML file to load if a region outside of any defined region map is selected. It is currently set to "NOREF." That simply means that nothing happens. It is OK to leave it like this. However, there are times when you may want to give the user some helpful or insulting feedback when he misses the map. Load a file named "badpick.htm." By naming it "badpick.htm" we are giving the user a chance to not click there. Remember, "badpick.htm" will appear in his browser's status line as he moves his pointer over this region.

So we change the file to:

```
<AREA SHAPE="default" HREF="badpick.htm" TARGET="INFO">
```

And we'll create an HTML file that lets the user know that it was a bad pick.
See Figure 7.7.

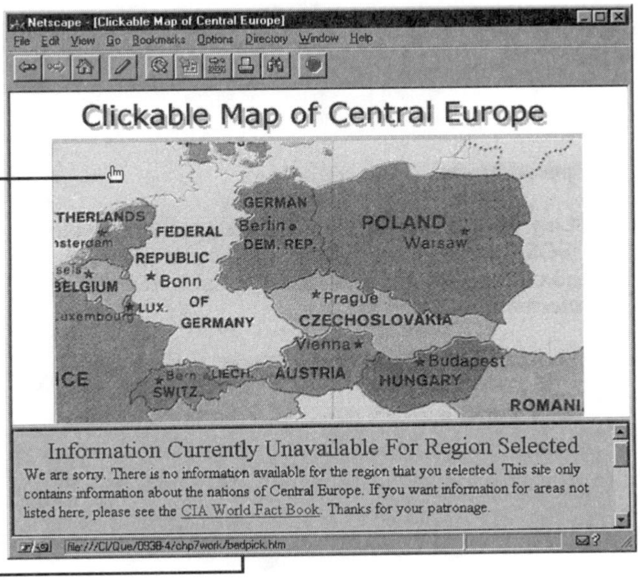

FIG. 7.7
You certainly don't
have to be rude. But
then again...

User in water,
undefined region

User alert for
bad pick

Where to Go from Here?

■ Chapter 4, "Using Frames Effectively"

Frames and image maps should go hand in hand for creating great-looking,
highly effective interactive content. Check out Chapter 4 for good information about frames.

■ Chapter 5, "Cool Effects with Images"

Trying to figure out what kind of image to use, or how to manipulate images?
See Chapter 5.

■ Shockwave Applet Ace

Shockwave Applet Ace has a Java applet especially designed for creating
clickable image maps. Applet Ace is contained on the CD. Although it isn't
the only way to deal with image maps, you might want to look at it. It's also a
nice example of Java at work.

Part
III

Ch
7

## CHAPTER 8

GIF Animations Are Fun and Easy

by Bray Jones

GIF animations are simply the best way to add excitement to your Web pages. There are other ways to add animations to Web pages, but none are as versatile, fast, or flexible. This chapter will focus on what GIF animations are, how they work, and how you can create them. ■

Defining GIF animations

GIF animations can be created because of special features built into the GIF89a format.

Adding GIF animations

Unlike other animations, a GIF animation is added simply by using an image tag.

Using builder programs

There are application programs for Mac and Windows that make the creation of GIF animations a snap.

Choosing a design program

3D animations, 2D-text animations, live animations, a series of completely unrelated frames that flash on screen—put a mini-movie on your site with GIF animation.

Setting the attributes

Speed, looping, transparency, the color palette, and so on, can all be modified within a GIF animation.

Looking at tips, tricks, and traps

There are many tips and tricks that really help juice up your animations. But, there are some traps to avoid also.

What Is a GIF Animation?

A GIF animation is a set of multiple images (frames) stored in a single file. GIF animations are created using the GIF89a standard and although the GIF89a standard has been around for almost 10 years and most graphical browsers support it, only a few support GIF animation. The browsers that don't support GIF animation only display the first image of the animation.

> **N O T E** You will likely hear more about the "PNG" image format in the future. It may very well replace the GIF format. For now, just think of PNG as GIF with more features (including real transparency and full color instead of the 256 limitation of GIF). PNG files do contain the ability to contain multiple images, so the capability for animation is preserved. Many of the tools described in this chapter will, no doubt, be updated to support the PNG format. You can learn more about PNG in Chapter 5, "Cool Effects with Images." ■

Advantages of GIF Animation

You will find most animations are done using the server push or client pull, in which the server has to send the data frame by frame to the client. This really tends to put a demanding load on the server, especially if it's a low-end server or lots of people are accessing it. The nice thing about GIF animations is once they are downloaded to your machine for viewing they are run from your local machine. So it's no different than downloading a standard GIF image. This is a great advantage over CGIs on the server because you can view and test your GIF animations directly from your local machine and don't have to work with your ISP (Internet Service Providers).

Some ISPs, from a security standpoint, won't let subscribers run their own CGIs or scripts, so this limits the number of individuals or companies that can produce animations via a CGI or script. Unless they operate their own Web servers, GIF animations are their best bet for animations.

GIF animations work across all platforms. They don't require a plug-in or a helper application to view them. No additional software other than your browser is needed.

Disadvantages of GIF Animation

As the title "GIF animation" implies, these are GIF files and therefore inherit the limitations of the GIF format. These limitations include:

■ GIF images have a color palette of only 256 colors.

Full-color images and particularly images that have been compressed by using JPEG compression may look very "blotchy" when converted to a 256-color format like GIF.

■ GIF animations do not play in all Web browsers.

GIF animations do play in Netscape Navigator, Microsoft Internet Explorer, and most other popular Web browsers. Nonsupporting GIF animation browsers either display the first or last image of the animation. With this in mind you want to make sure both the first and last frame of your animation is something that is viewable and relates to the theme of the animation.

■ The GIF animation cannot be used as a background image.

Not a tremendous drawback because reading text over an animation just might be a little bit difficult.

■ There is no file protection available for GIF animations.

This means that your animations can be copied and used by anyone who can view your Web page.

How to Add GIF Animations to Your Page

Adding a GIF animation to your Web page is as simple as adding a graphic image. Below are a few examples of how you might use the image (IMG) tag to load a GIF animation.

```
<IMG SRC="Walking.gif">
```

This is the basic IMG tag. This example will load the image "Walking.gif" while the rest of your Web page loads.

```
<IMG SRC="Walking.gif" ALT="Walking Man">
```

Adding the ALT attribute adds a text description of the image. This text is then displayed when the image is "broken" or your client is a text-only browser.

```
<IMG SRC="Walking.gif" LOWSRC="Walk.gif" ALT="Walking Man">
```

The LOWSRC attribute lets you load the image "Walk.gif" before the SRC image. This image is typically small, so it loads fast and gives the user something to look at before the SRC image is loaded.

```
<IMG SRC="Walking.gif" LOWSRC="Walk.gif" ALT="Walking Man"
HEIGHT=40 WIDTH=30>
```

The HEIGHT and WIDTH attribute specifies the intended height and width of the image in pixels. This lets the browsers reserve screen space for the image before the image is loaded.

GIF Animation Builder Programs

There are plenty of programs that assemble the sequence of GIFs for an animation. They are available for both the Macintosh and Windows platform and most are either freeware or shareware. Some work better than others and have more options for controlling the animation, so you may want to take a look at a few and find one that you feel comfortable with.

A Few GIF Animation Builders

The following are some applications that can be used to build GIF animations:

- GifBuilder (Macintosh)

  http://iawww.epfl.ch/Staff/Yves.Piguet/clip2gif-home/ GifBuilder.html

- GIF Construction Set (Windows 3.1, Win95, and Windows NT)

  http://www.mindworkshop.com

- Graphic Converter by Thorsten Lemke (Macintosh and Windows)

  This is available through a number of sites that provide access to freeware and shareware applications, including **http://www.tucows.com**

- GIFMerge (Unix)

  http://www.iis.ee.ethz.ch/~kiwi/GIFMerge/

Creating a Sample GIF Animation

In this example, you learn how to create a simple neon sign effect with text. See Figure 8.1. This should get you familiar with how to create the images, import the images into your GIF-building program, use the attributes to control the animation, and save the animation as a GIF animation.

FIG. 8.1
Create the image.

Step I—Creating the Initial Image

1. Start your favorite paint program and open a new window.

2. Make the background color of your document the same color as the BGCOLOR of your HTML document.

   In this example, the background color is set to white.

3. Create a word with the text tool.

4. Blur the text by one or two pixels.

5. Save the image as 01.gif. Macintosh users need to save the file as 01.pict.

Step II—Creating Individual Images for the Animation   In the previous section, you completed a few steps to create a GIF image. The following steps tell you how to create different frames from the same image.

1. Select all but the first character of the text of the GIF image you created, as shown in Figure 8.2.

FIG. 8.2
Selecting characters
for modification.

2. Increase the brightness by 100 percent and the contrast by 30 percent. This will make the letters selected a little washed out and dim. This creates the affect of the first letter "turning on" in the neon sign. Save this image as 02.gif. Again, Macintosh users need to save the image as 02.pict.

3. With the original image (01.gif), select all but the first two letters and repeat step 6. Save this image as 03.pict. Do this with the rest of the letters, eventually turning all the letters on. Name the file in numeric order. The last picture

should be the one with all the letters "turned off." See Figure 8.3, which shows the resulting images on a Macintosh platform.

FIG. 8.3
Five frames have been created from one image.

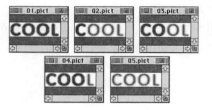

Step III—Importing the Images as Frames   In the previous section, you completed a few steps to create the series of images that you use to create your animation. The following steps tell you how to import and rearrange the frames in a GIF-building program, such as GIF Builder for the Macintosh. Other GIF-building programs on other platforms let you import the frames into their programs in a similar way.

1. Now you can import the frames you created by opening your GIF-building program and creating a new document.

2. Import or add the images you've created into the new window. Sort them by name. That's where the numeric ordering comes in handy. See Figure 8.4 for the resulting list for a Macintosh user.

FIG. 8.4
Import the images.

Frames					
5 frames	Length: 0.50 s	Size: (105×31)			No loop
Name	Size	Position	Disp.	Delay	Transp.
01.pict	105×31	(0; 0)	N	10	–
02.pict	105×31	(0; 0)	N	10	–
03.pict	105×31	(0; 0)	N	10	–
04.pict	105×31	(0; 0)	N	10	–
05.pict	105×31	(0; 0)	N	10	–

If you are on a different platform, such as Windows, your list should show 01.GIF, 02.GIF, 03.GIF, and so on.

3. Duplicate the first frame, and move it in front of the last frame. This step will give you a fully "turned on" frame before the last frame turns it off.

4. Duplicate the last frame and move it to after the first frame. This step turns the frame fully "off" before the sign starts to come on. Figure 8.5 shows the resulting frames for a Macintosh user.

FIG. 8.5
Duplicate frames that
will be used again.

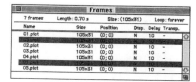

Step IV—Setting GIF Animation Attributes and Saving the GIF Animation. Since
we now have all the frames arranged properly we need to set some attributes that
make them fit the theme of a NEON sign. Remember, each GIF-building program
may call the same attributes different names.

1. Turn the looping attribute on "Forever." On the Windows platform, you
   might have to set the iterations to some high number, as shown in Figure 8.6.

FIG. 8.6
Turn looping on.

2. Select all the frames and set the Interframe delay to 50/100 seconds (half a
   second). See Figure 8.7. The default delay of 10/100 seconds is too fast for a
   neon sign.

FIG. 8.7
Set the Interframe
delay.

3. Set the color palette to Best Palette if you're using a Macintosh. GIF Construction Set (Windows) may call this option "Edit Image/Palette," as shown in
   Figure 8.8. If you're using UNIX, it may be called "Best Guess Palette." Whatever the case, this will let the GIF-building program determine the best set of
   256 colors from all the frames in the animation. Also, if you have created your
   own color palette for your animation, then you may load it instead.

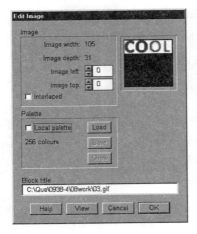

FIG. 8.8
Select the color palette.

4. Turn interlacing off. You don't want your frames progressively showing up on the screen. It slows your animation down and makes it unviewable.

5. Turn Frame Optimization on. This option will crop and keep only the changes from frame to frame and display them over the previous frame. In this case, we reduced the final size from 7k to 5k by turning Frame Optimization on. Some GIF-building programs might not have a "Frame Optimization" option or it might be called something different.

6. Save the GIF animation. You can embed this animation in your HTML document for viewing with the image tag, explained in the section, "How to Add GIF Animations to Your Web Page," earlier in this chapter.

Choosing a Program to Design Your GIF Animation

There are many different ways to design/create your GIF animation. From the basic drawing package to the high-end 3D program to the QuickTime Movie editing program. No matter what you create the frames in, they can all be exported as images that can be used to create a GIF animation.

Drawing/Paint Program

This is your standard pixel-based paint program (Adobe Photoshop, for instance). This allows you lots of flexibility when creating a GIF animation because you can control every detail of the picture before you save it as a pict or GIF. Some GIF-building programs even recognize the Adobe Photoshop 3.0 format and will import the file and place each layer of the Photoshop file into a different frame. This saves you from having to save each layer as a pict or GIF file, then importing it into the GIF-building program. Other simple paint programs can be used as long as they can save pict or GIF file formats.

3D-Rendering Programs

3D programs are nice when you want to create some realistic high-quality rendered effects like a sphere mapped with a mirror texture that reflects its surroundings. Spinning logos are a popular effect created in 3D programs. Usually, the price of a 3D program is a little steep for the average user, but some really neat GIF animations can be created if you have a 3D program and know how to use it. All 3D programs will export the animation of your 3D objects to a QuickTime movie or a series of PICS that you can easily import into your favorite GIF-building program.

Movie Editing Programs

You can create some really neat Hollywood style movie effects if you use a program like Adobe Premiere and Macromind Director. Different transitions between frames can be controlled or text can be transitioned in softly over a picture you have displayed. If you are not familiar with movie editing programs, it may take you awhile to learn the features. Once you do, you can produce nice special effects that can be easily made into a GIF animation.

How to Set the Attributes that Affect GIF Animations

The GIF89a format has a set of attributes that controls GIF animations. These attributes are controllable from most of the popular GIF animation builders. Below is a brief description of the attributes used to control GIF animations.

Looping

The Loop attribute lets you set how many times the animation is repeated. Most of the time you have the option to specify no loop, loop x amount of times, or loop forever. Some browsers don't acknowledge the loop attribute and others may loop forever if it's set to a value greater than one. Some programs may call the looping effect different names, such as "Loop Block" or "Iterations."

N O T E   Some people don't like GIF animations that loop forever, especially if you have several animations on one page. It tends to slow other things down a bit and can become somewhat annoying after awhile, depending on the animation. ■

Interlacing

Interlacing allows your image to be drawn on the screen progressively in four stages with each frame. This is fine for standard GIFs but is not recommended for animation. It slows your animation down and distorts the effect of your animation.

Colors and Depth

As with standard GIFs, by keeping the number of colors to a minimum you reduce the file size and thus make your downloading of GIFs quicker. The same goes for animation. Some GIF animation builders let you choose predetermined palettes like the system palette or a grayscale palette. Also, you may let the program itself determine the best palette for that particular animation based on all of the frames loaded. You can also load an existing color palette if there are a set of colors you want to use instead. A 6×6×6 palette may be available in some programs, giving you the ability use colors that "map" across platforms. This is the palette that Netscape for Windows uses. A few programs will even remove unused colors from your palette, thereby reducing the palette and file size of the animation.

Dithering

Dithering is when the computer can't find the color a pixel calls for, so it changes the adjacent pixels to trick the human eye into thinking it's the right color. Dithering is useful for displays that cannot represent full color and for file formats, like

GIF, that only support 256 colors. The best time to use dithering is if you have a continuous ban of colors.

Transparent Color

If you use the Transparent Color attribute, you can specify a color that will be invisible, and the background color of the browser will show through. Most programs let you specify a transparency color.

Interframe Delay

This enables you to specify a delay between the current frame and the next frame. It's usually specified in hundredths of seconds(100 means 1 second). Strategically using the interframe delay can save you from needing to duplicate frames one after the other to lengthen an animation or provide a pause before the next frame.

N O T E Using the As Fast As Possible option can yield unpredictably fast speeds depending on how fast your computer is. ■

Disposal Method

The Disposal Method determines what happens to the frame after the interframe delay has elapsed. There are currently four options to choose from. They are the following:

- Unspecified—Does nothing with the current frame. The next frame overwrites the current frame.

- Do Not Dispose—Overlays certain data of the next frame over the current frame. This option is selected if you have frame optimization turned on. This lets only data that has changed from the next frame be layed over the current frame. This keeps from having to load duplicate data for the next frame because it just keeps that data in place and overlays the new changes, thus reducing the frame size and total animation size. In some cases, this results in a large file size reduction.

- Revert to Background—Reverts to the current background before the next frame is loaded. Use this option when you have transparency set. Some browsers do not support this option.

■ Revert to Previous—This option may be used if you have objects moving across the animation that are overlayed over a larger, previous frame.

Background Color

The Background Color is the color used when you don't have a frame displayed. Some browsers ignore this option and display the current background of the page. A good rule of thumb is to make the backgrounds of your animations the same color as the background used in your HTML page, so when the animation plays, the color of the animation background is the same as the browser background.

Frame Position

This option lets you specify an amount each frame can be shifted by. You can specify the vertical and horizontal distance (in pixels) between the top left frame corner and the top left corner of the animation.

Tips, Tricks, and Traps with GIF Animation

The following is my bag of tips, tricks, and traps. As you create more and more GIF animations you will find your own as well.

Utilize the Frame Position Attribute

Using the Frame Position attribute in a GIF animation can save you lots of time and painstaking cropping and saving of images. Creating an effect like an electronic sign that scrolls the text from right to left can utilize the Frame Position attribute to do all the work for you. The scrolling "Hello" in Figure 8.9 has actually changed in size from the default 250×20 to 70×20. This lets you look through a "window," where you can see only 75 vertical pixels of the image at once. Each time an additional 20 pixels from the previous frame is added, the frame position is offset. This makes the frame itself seem to "move" to the left. Figure 8.10 shows the results of using a single image to simulate a moving, electronic sign.

FIG. 8.9
This single "Hello" image was used to create a scrolling GIF animation. It was just used eight times.

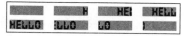

FIG. 8.10
The electronic sign in motion!

Let the Interframe Delay Attribute Work for You

An interframe delay in the first frame of an image gives the frame a nice pause before the next frame that starts the animation. By putting the pause (interframe delay) at the top where there is a blank frame, you don't have to add an extra frame at the end of the animation just for the sake of a pause. This cuts out one frame from the animation and reduces the animation size.

Play with the Bit Depth

Try different settings with the bit depth on your GIF animation. Often, you will find that by lowering the bit depth you don't really lose any clarity but save some download time by reducing the file size.

Frame Optimization Can Reduce Your Animation Size

The Frame Optimization option will look at the difference between the current frame and the next frame and will keep only the portion that has changed. It overlays that changed part over the current frame. In some cases, this will drastically reduce your file size. This option should be used with Do Not Dispose selected for the Disposal Method. Remember, Frame Optimization may not be supported by the GIF-building program you use, or it may be called something else.

Utilize the LOWSRC Attribute in the IMG Tag

```
<IMG SRC="Walking.gif" LOWSRC="Walk.gif">
```

If you have large (greater than 50k) GIF animations on your Web site, try the LOWSRC attribute on the IMG tag to load a small GIF (usually a GIF of the first frame) before the SRC image is loaded. By loading the LOWSRC image first this will serve as a placeholder and something to look at while the GIF animation is loading.

Use Height and Width Attributes to Reserve Space on Your Web Page

```
<IMG SRC="Walking.gif" HEIGHT=40 WIDTH=60>
```

By utilizing the HEIGHT and WIDTH attributes with your GIF animations as well as regular GIFs, you can have the text of your Web page load before your graphics. This gives the user something to read as your graphics load. Have you ever seen a page background load, then it takes a minute or two before the whole page loads? If they had used the HEIGHT and WIDTH attributes, the user wouldn't have had to wait. The text would have loaded and the HEIGHT and WIDTH attributes would preserve the space needed for the graphics that load in later.

Using QuickTime Movies to Make a GIF Animation Is Easy

Basically the GIF animation is created if your source for your animation is a QuickTime movie. Most GIF-building programs will import QuickTime movies with each frame in the movie as a frame in the animation. Just set the attributes of the movie (palette, looping, and so on), save the file, and that's it—instant GIF animations.

Don't Rely on the GIF-Builder Program's Preview Mode

Some GIF builders will let you preview your animation before you save it as a GIF animation. Nothing replaces viewing the animation in the browser itself. Always test your animations with your browser (or several browsers if you have access to them) before placing them on the Web. Sometimes, the preview mode in the GIF-builder program just doesn't look the same as in the browser.

Place Duplicate GIF Animations Side by Side to Create Random Affects

Looking at Figures 8.11 and 8.12 below you can see that by duplicating the same small animation (6-10 frames) four times and placing them side by side with the image tag you can simulate some random effects. By using duplicate copies, the computer itself will update the animations at different times because the computer is also busy doing other things.

FIG. 8.11
Here are three separate instances of the same four GIF animations placed side by side in the image tags:

```
<IMG SRC="LED.gif"> <IMG SRC="LED.gif"> <IMG SRC="LED.gif"> <IMG
SRC="LED.gif">
```

FIG. 8.12
Here are three separate instances of the same "LED.gif" animation duplicated four times and referenced individually in the image tags:

```
<IMG SRC="LED1.gif"> <IMG SRC="LED2.gif"> <IMG SRC="LED3.gif"> <IMG
SRC="LED4.gif">
```

Remember the Modem Speed of Your Users

Test your GIF animations on the server you have your Web page on. If the speed of downloading the GIF animation seems too slow for you, then it's probably too slow for everyone else, too. Go back and make some modifications to it. You could remove some frames that are really not needed, for instance. Check to see if you can use the interframe delay option instead of duplicate frames to create a pause if you need one. Lower your bit depth and see if you can live with the reduction in colors. Turn on Frame Optimization.

Do NOT Overcrowd Your Web Pages with GIF Animations

You shouldn't have more than two or three GIF animations on a page if they are medium size (30-40k). You can have a few more if they are small (less than 30k). Large GIF animations (greater than 50k) that take time to download might have the user clicking the back button because it's just taking too long to load the page. Limit your frames to no more than 25 if they are small, 10-15 if medium size, and 5-10 if large.

Use GIF Animations to Build Dynamic Bar Charts

You normally see graphed data displayed as a GIF file. Take the raw data and build your bar chart graph automatically. See the bar chart GIF animation in Figure 8.13.

FIG. 8.13
First you need to build your GIF animations to animate the bars in the bar chart. The figure shows twenty different GIF animations. The tallest GIF (BAR20.gif) is an animation made up of the previous 19 bars. The next to the tallest GIF (BAR19.gif) is made up of the previous 18 bars, and so on.

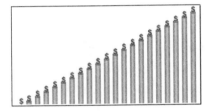

Figure 8.14 is charting the FY95 sales (in millions of dollars) for each month. The maximum amount in sales is $100 Million. To calculate which GIF animation you will need for a particular month, take the sales in millions (for instance, $86.2 Million) and multiply it by two. The reason will be explained in a moment. Take the 172.6 and divide it by 10 to calculate to 17.4. Now round the 17.4 to 17. You will use "BAR17.gif" to represent $86.2 Million dollars.

If you had 100 GIF animations to represent $1 million to $100 million, then you would have a one to one correlation. Since you only have 20 GIF animations to represent $1 million to $100 million, you have a one to five correlation. To make that correct you have to multiply the amount by two. Now, you have to take that number and divide it by 10, so you'll have a whole number that "maps" to the correct GIF animation.

Try to figure out how you want to "map" your GIF animations to your values. A one to one relation is best, but that means you have to create that many animations as well. It gets very tiresome to create 100 GIF animations. So only create half as many (or a fourth as many) and divide your value by 2 or 4.

FIG. 8.14
Here is a sample of what the final bar chart would look like. Remember each bar would be a GIF animation and would animate the bar growing until it reached the correct dollar value. The HTML code for this example is shown below.

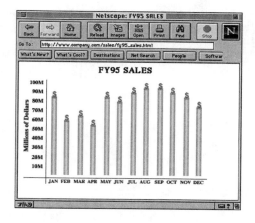

```
<HTML><TITLE>FY95 SALES</TITLE>
<BODY BGCOLOR="#FFFFFF" TEXT="#000000">
<H2><center>FY95 SALES</center></H2>
<IMG SRC="Dollars.gifÓ>
<IMG SRC="BAR17.GIF" HSPACE=1><IMG SRC="BAR12.GIF" HSPACE=1>
<IMG SRC="BAR13.GIF" HSPACE=1><IMG SRC="BAR11.GIF" HSPACE=1>
<IMG SRC="BAR17.GIF" HSPACE=1><IMG SRC="BAR16.GIF" HSPACE=1>
<IMG SRC="BAR18.GIF" HSPACE=1><IMG SRC="BAR19.GIF" HSPACE=1>
<IMG SRC="BAR19.GIF" HSPACE=1><IMG SRC="BAR18.GIF" HSPACE=1>
<IMG SRC="BAR17.GIF" HSPACE=1><IMG SRC="BAR15.GIF" HSPACE=1>
<br>
<IMG SRC="Months.gif">
</BODY>
</HTML>
```

The HSPACE attribute will space out the animations by one pixel. Use this attribute to space the bars equally or place the animations in a table.

Let Your Imagination Run Wild

You can look at almost any Web site and see some type of GIF animation. Anyone can create text animations that spell out a message or animate a stick man walking in place. But what really blows people away is something they've never seen before, such as the "rotating-head" animation in Figure 8.15.

FIG. 8.15
Take this last example. It was made using a video camcorder, a swivel chair, a Macintosh Quadra 660AV, and Adobe Photoshop 3.0.5. A total of 26 frames were used to generate this rotating-head animation. Only eight of the 26 are shown.

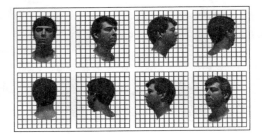

How the Rotating Head Was Created

The following is a description of how the rotating-head animation was created.

First, the subject set up his camcorder on a tripod connected to an AV (Audio Video) Macintosh, so he could see what the camcorder was viewing without having to look in the viewfinder. He sat down in a swivel chair about 10 feet away and positioned his head correctly in the camera window. His backdrop was just a plain white wall. He wore a tank top that was a different color than white, so he could easily edit it out to make his neck lines clean and simulate his head floating. He turned the camcorder on and moved slowly around in the chair, trying to keep his head completely steady in the same X, Y, and Z axis. After a few turns (takes) he went back to the Mac to save them to disk as a QuickTime movie at 10 frames per second.

He imported half of the frames (one half turn) from the QuickTime movie as layers into Adobe Photoshop. He only imported half of the frames, because the other half of the turn he could make by flipping horizontally the first half of the movie. This made the frames line up evenly. He edited out the background and tank top from each frame. He added a grid to the background, so each frame would overlay on top of it. It gave it more of a digital finish. He used GIFBuilder for the Macintosh to create the GIF animation with looping turned on so his head would spin forever. It only took him a few hours to do this, and the results looked like his head was actually scanned in with one of those high-end laser scanners used for Hollywood special effects. See what a little imagination can do.

Where to Go from Here?

- Chapter 5, "Cool Effects with Images"

  Provides information on how to create images suitable for Web browsing.

- Chapter 9, "Attract Attention with Dynamic Pages"

  Contains some shortcuts for creating quick and easy animations.

- Chapter 12, "All that Shockwave"

  Provides information on the Macromedia products, many of which can help you create sophisticated animations.

- Chapter 14, "Java, Cookies, and Other Tricks"

  Provides an example of using an applet to create an animation.

- Chapter 15, "CGI Scripts - Practically Cut-and-Paste City"

  Gets you started with CGI scripts, including a "server-push," which lets you add animations to your Web pages.

- The CD-ROM

  Provides GIF animation tools, CGI scripts, and Java applets that you can use to create animations.

- **http://members.aol.com/royalef/gallery.htm** and **http:// www.groupz.net/~bray**

  Supplies samples of GIF animations.

## CHAPTER 9

Attract Attention with Dynamic Pages

There are a variety of methods you can use to add animations to your Web pages. Creating GIF animations is described in Chapter 8, "GIF Animations Are Fun and Easy" (if you haven't checked it out, go there now). In this chapter, you cover the other methods you can use to create exciting, graphically dynamic Web pages. ▪

How to use scrolling text

Scrolling text is the easiest type of animation that can be added to your page—easy but annoying if overused. You can add it to your pages with JavaScript or by using the <MARQUEE> tag.

How to use client-side pull

You can send information to your client that gives it the name of the *next* file to be loaded. You can either keep loading the same HTML file or load any one that you want (as long as you know its complete URL).

How to use server-side push

This is the oldest way of getting animation on your Web page (well, maybe second oldest; swirling your mouse around really fast might count, too).

How to use a Java applet for animation

Java applets provide a plethora of capabilities to browsers. Here, you look at how we can use one specific applet to add animation to your Web page.

Moving Text Is Easy Animation

If you have some late-breaking news, you will probably want to bring attention to it. And, rather than use the (God forbid) <BLINK> tag, there are more intelligent ways to get your viewers' attention. One of those quick tricks is scrolling text.

Scrolling Text by Using JavaScript

Netscape Navigator and Internet Explorer both support JavaScript. This lets you do all kinds of special effects and add all kinds of functionality to your HTML documents. Fortunately, for a script like scrolling text, you can find prebuilt versions that work very well. Listing 9.1 is JavaScript code that adds scrolling text to the bottom of your browser window, as seen in Figure 9.1.

FIG. 9.1
Scrolling text added to the status bar along the bottom of the browser window.

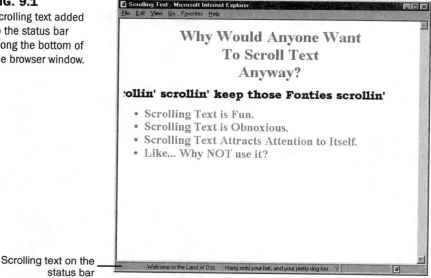

Scrolling text on the status bar

Listing 9.1   The Scrolling Text JavaScript

```
<HTML>
<HEAD>
<TITLE>Scrolling Text(/TITLE>
<SCRIPT LANGUAGE="JavaScript">
<!-- Beginning of JavaScript Applet -----------------
```

```
/* Copyright (C)1996 Web Integration Systems, Inc. DBA Websys, Inc.
   All Rights Reserved.
   This applet can be re-used or modified, if credit is given in
   the source code.

   We will not be held responsible for any unwanted effects due to the
   usage of this applet or any derivative.  No warrantees for usability
   for any specific application are given or implied.

   Chris Skinner, January 30th, 1996.
*/

function scrollit_r2l(seed)
{
        var m1  = "one ";
        var m2  = "two ";
        var m3  = "three ";
        var m4  = "";

        var msg=m1+m2+m3+m4;
        var out = " ";
        var c   = 1;

        if (seed > 100) {
                seed--;
                var cmd="scrollit_r2l(" + seed + ")";
                timerTwo=window.setTimeout(cmd,100);
        }
        else if (seed <= 100 && seed > 0) {
                for (c=0 ; c < seed ; c++) {
                        out+=" ";
                }
                out+=msg;
                seed--;
                var cmd="scrollit_r2l(" + seed + ")";
                    window.status=out;
                timerTwo=window.setTimeout(cmd,100);
        }
        else if (seed <= 0) {
                if (-seed < msg.length) {
                        out+=msg.substring(-seed,msg.length);
                        seed--;
                        var cmd="scrollit_r2l(" + seed + ")";
                        window.status=out;
                        timerTwo=window.setTimeout(cmd,100);
                }
                else {
                        window.status=" ";
                        timerTwo=window.setTimeout("scrollit_r2l(100)",
                        ➡75);
                }
```

continues

Listing 9.1 Continued

```
        }
}
// -- End of JavaScript code ------------- -->
</SCRIPT>
</HEAD>
<BODY onLoad="timerONE=window.setTimeout('scrollit_r2l(100)',500);"
BGCOLOR=#FFFFFF>
```

The parts of the script you want to modify are located near the top of the script and are shown in the following code. Each of the "var" statements defines a variable that you can adjust.

```
        var m1  = "one ";
        var m2  = "two ";
        var m3  = "three ";
        var m4  = "";
You can modify these variables to present any message that you would
➥like to the end user:
var m1  = "Welcome to the land of Ozz.   ";
        var m2  = "I hope that you find what you are looking for.  ";
        var m3  = "Please watch your step. and remember to follow the
➥yellow brick road";
        var m4  = "";
```

You then should place the entire JavaScript, with these modified variables, between the <HEAD> and </HEAD> tags. Make sure the <BODY> tag includes the command to get the whole process off and running. You can see the result in Figure 9.1.

Internet Explorer's Marquee

Internet Explorer has the <MARQUEE> tag extension. Marquee lets you scroll any text that you want across your screen. It has several options but can be quickly added to your screen simply by adding the tag.

<MARQUEE>This text will scroll like crazy...</MARQUEE>

By default the text will scroll from right to left (I guess that's so you can hold your eyes still while the text flies by, and you can still read it from left to right). This effect can be quite alarming, as demonstrated in Figure 9.2.

And of course you can get a little fancier, as demonstrated in the following code.

```
<H2><FONT FACE="COMIC SANS MS">
<MARQUEE WIDTH=95%>
Scrollin' scrollin' scrollin' keep those Fonties scrollin'...
</MARQUEE>
</FONT></H2>
```

FIG. 9.2
You can specify both a scrolling JavaScript and a MARQUEE. How's that for a busy page?

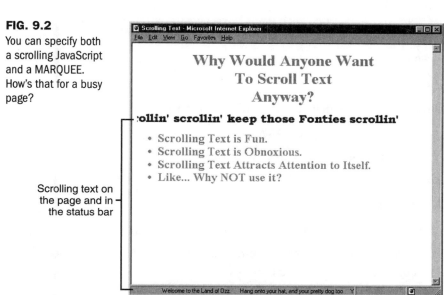

Scrolling text on the page and in the status bar

Clients Pull You into the Future

Client pull lets you automate HTML loading by the browser. You can use this feature to create slide shows or other effects. You create a client pull by simply putting a directive in the HEAD of an HTML file.

Delivering Dynamic Hockey Scores (or other less important info)

Let's say you have some information that changes regularly, like stock market quotes or hockey scores. And, for some reason, you want to continually update this information for users. Client pull provides you with a simple mechanism to continually update the user's browser. The following example will work:

```
<HTML>
<HEAD>
<META HTTP-EQUIV="Refresh" CONTENT=600>
<TITLE>Hockey Scoreboard</TITLE>
</HEAD>
<BODY>
<H2>Redwings vs. Avalanche</H2>
At 13:15 of the 1st period, the score is:
<P><FONT SIZE=4><BLINK>Detroit 6 Colorado 0</BLINK></FONT>
<H2>Penguins vs. Rangers</H2>
FINAL:
<P><FONT SIZE=4><BLINK>Pittsburg 1 New York 2</BLINK></FONT>
</BODY>
<HTML>
```

There are only two things that you have to do in order for this to work.

■ Include the META tag in the HEAD.

■ Update the scores regularly on your server.

In this example:

```
<META HTTP-EQUIV="Refresh" CONTENT=600>
```

Refresh—shows that this document should be reloaded.

CONTENT—specifies (in seconds) how frequently the document should be reloaded, in this case every 10 minutes.

Now, all you have to do is figure out how to capture this data automatically (by writing a CGI script, for example), and you'll have a cool page that folks will keep right on their desktops!

TIP   It's the end of the day, and all scores are in. Just remove the META tag from the HEAD; this HTML will download after this modification and, without a "refresh" command, the document will then become static.

The Never-Ending Slide Show

You can also use client pull to put together a continuously running slide show. You simply need to provide an URL for the next HTML document that you want to load in the HEAD of the HTML documents. Remember HTTP-EQUIV specifies the next HTML document that you want loaded.

<META HTTP-EQUIV="Refresh" CONTENT="0; URL=http://www.r.y/
page1.html">

> **CAUTION**
>
> Make sure you give the complete URL of the document that you want to link to.

Here are three example documents: page1.html, page2.html, and page3.html.
page1.html loads page2.html. page2.html loads page3.html. page3.html loads
page1.html. This creates a perpetual motion machine! See Listings 9.2, 9.3, and 9.4.

Listing 9.2   The HTML Specification for Page 1

```
<HTML>
<HEAD>
<META HTTP-EQUIV=REFRESH CONTENT="0; URL=http://.../page2.html">
<TITLE>Page One</TITLE>
</HEAD>
<BODY>
<H2>This is Page 1</H2>
One is the lonliest number that I've ever seen.
</BODY>
</HTML>
```

Listing 9.3   The HTML Specification for Page 2

```
<HTML>
<HEAD>
<META HTTP-EQUIV=REFRESH CONTENT="0; URL=http://.../page3.html">
<TITLE>Page Two</TITLE>
</HEAD>
<BODY>
<H2>This is Page 2</H2>
Two is Company.
</BODY>
</HTML>
```

Listing 9.4   The HTML Specification for Page 3

```
<HTML>
<HEAD>
<META HTTP-EQUIV=REFRESH CONTENT="0; URL=http://.../page1.html">
<TITLE>Page Three</TITLE>
</HEAD>
<BODY>
<H2>This is Page 3</H2>
Three's a Crowd!
</BODY>
</HTML>
```

 You can set CONTENT="0" to any time that you like. Setting to "0" assures that the entire page loads before the next page loads. If you want to set this to any other interval, make sure you allow enough time for the next document to download, or you'll blast right off to another document before the current document is fully downloaded.

Of course, there is no reason to loop your slide show. You can simply leave out the META tag in the last document and the slide show will halt.

Push Those Graphics

Before GIF animations became popular, almost all animations that you saw on the Web were server-side pushes. A server-side push can occur when the server never really closes down its connection with the client. This trick lets the server send images one after another to the client even after the client has received all other information.

You need the following to get server push to work:

- A series of images, all of the same resolution and format, that you want to animate. Either GIF or JPEG images are fine.
- Specify these images and other attributes in the nph-anim.pl script.

   You can specify which images play, and how many times they play.

- Put the nph-anim.pl script in your server's cgi-bin directory.

  For this particular script to work you need access to your server's cgi-bin directory. If this is not possible, your service provider probably has a server push application that you can use. The only problem is that setting the pusher's variables (like image names and number of times played) will have to be available to the pusher from another file. This will just take a little longer to get through (those GIF animations are starting to look better already, aren't they).

- Make room for your animation in an HTML document.

  This looks pretty much like a standard HTML image tag.

> **N O T E**   For more general information about modifying, adjusting, and creating CGI scripts, please see Chapter 15, "CGI Scripts." ■

Step 1—Get the Images

Get the images from any source that you want, a series of line drawings or digitized video images. It doesn't really matter. You should concern yourself with image size. See Chapter 5, "Cool Effects with Images," for information about reducing the sizes of images effectively.

Step 2—Modify the Script

Open the file named "nph-anim.pl" in a text editor. You will see a "variable" section marked off near the top of the page. See the following code. The only things that you have to modify are these few variables.

```
# Variables
$times = "1";
$basefile = "/WWW/images/animation/";
@files = ("begin.gif","second.gif","third.gif","last.gif");
$con_type = "gif";
# Done
```

$times—specifies the number of times that you want the animation to loop. "1" plays the animation once. "2" plays the animation twice, and so on.

If you want the animation to loop three times, set it to:

```
$times = "3";
```

$basefile—specifies the full path to the directory, where the images will be found.

If the home directory is **www.cris.com/~tlockwoo**, store the images in a directory named "graphx"; so this line will look like:

```
$basefile = "/www.cris.com/~tlockwoo/graphx/";
```

@files—specifies the actual names of the images in the order that you want them played.

The files are named "step01.jpg" through "step10.jpg". This line will look like:

```
@files = ("step01.jpeg", "step02.jpeg", "step03.jpeg", "step04.jpeg",
➡"step05.jpeg", "step06.jpeg", "step07.jpeg", "step08.jpeg",
➡"step09.jpeg", "step10.jpeg");
```

TIP Some server-push scripts play the image files alphabetically; therefore, it doesn't hurt to name them so they play correctly. In the previous example, you can see that a zero has been added before the last digit of numbers less than "10."

$con_type—specifies the type of image that is being pushed, normally "GIF" or "JPEG".

My files are JPEGs, so this is easy:

```
$con_type = "jpeg";
```

That's it. When you're done, you have a section in nph-anim.pl that looks like the following.

```
# Variables
$times = "3";
$basefile = "www.cris.com/~tlockwoo/graphx/";
@files = ("step01.jpeg", "step02.jpeg", "step03.jpeg", "step04.jpeg",
➡"step05.jpeg", "step06.jpeg", "step07.jpeg", "step08.jpeg",
➡"step09.jpeg", "step10.jpeg");
$con_type = "jpeg";
# Done
```

Pretty easy.

Step 3—Put Your Proud New Script on Your Server

Just FTP this script to your cgi-bin directory. While you're doing that, make sure you notice where the "cgi-bin" directory is. It can be off the root, or on some servers; you may even have one, for your use, in your own directory.

> **CAUTION**
>
> Your cgi-bin directory is a special directory. You cannot just create a directory named "cgi-bin" and expect it to work. If you cannot find the cgi-bin directory, contact your system administrator to find out where it is and how you can gain access to it.

Part
III

Ch
9

Step 4—Make Room in Your Favorite HTML File

You now add a reference to this script where you want the images to appear in your HTML file. Just add the name of your script's URL.

<IMG SRC="http://www.name.com/cgi-bin/npl-anim.pl">

Of course, you can then add image attributes just like you would for any other image. For example:

<IMG SRC="http://www.cris.com/cgi-bin/npl-anim.pl" ALIGN=CENTER VSPACE=10 BORDER=0 ALT="Dude Walking">.

> **N O T E** If this is the first CGI script that you have worked with, you are bound to make a few mistakes along the way. Remember, HTML wasn't all that easy at first, either. Don't overlook the obvious, and before you get too frustrated, e-mail your service provider for some hints or tips. They probably even have some online help. This is a very common task to want to accomplish and has been around for awhile, so you won't surprise anyone by asking some questions. ▪

Animate with Java

Java is the hottest topic on the Internet right now. Why? Java provides a relatively sophisticated programming language that lets the executable files be downloaded to your browser and run locally. This opens completely new horizons for the kinds of things that you can experience within the confines of your browser. More about Java in Chapter 14, "Java, Cookies, and Other Tricks." In this chapter, we want to confine our discussion to one particular applet that is available on the CD; this applet lets you add animation to your pages with a lot of control, and they run great, too. See Figure 9.3 for some animated coffee beans.

FIG. 9.3
Now, I just need some Cookies and a Visual Cafe!

How to Use Applets—Easy as Pie

There is a little setup to get an applet to run correctly. For the most part, it involves making sure that things are in the right place. Now, how to install your applet:

1. Make a copy of the sample applet.

   Or remember where you got the applet. When you mess it up you will want to get another copy quickly. Don't mess with the applet's directory structure until you have tested it and know how you want to modify it.

2. Open the HTML file in your browser to make sure that it works.

   Usually applets come with HTML files as examples. These are usually named things like "example.html", "test.html" or "appletname.html". Just open them up with your browser to make sure they work.

3. Replace the images used for the sample animation with your images.

Read through the applet documentation. Make sure that your images are in the correct format. The documentation will also let you know if you can have different size images or not, whether you can mix image formats, and other important information. Figure 9.3 shows a sample page of comments. This makes modifying the applet very easy.

4. Insert the applet into your HTML document.

Put your HTML document into the same directory as the example HTML file that you just tested. Open the example in a text editor, and open your HTML document in a text editor. Copy the entire applet and paste it into your HTML document.

5. Test it again.

Open your HTML document with the browser, and make sure it works with your new images.

6. Adjust the parameters as desired.

Most applets have a rich set of user-definable parameters. Note: all parameters may not be used in the example HTML file that you used, as seen in Figure 9.3.

FIG. 9.4
Applets can be very well documented, which makes installing them very easy.

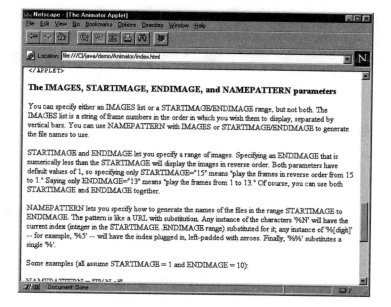

7. Test.

   How frequently you test depends on how sure you are that you are going to make a bunch of mistakes. It's better to test one or two parameters at a time so that you don't forget what you're doing.

8. Place the applet on your server (if necessary).

   If the applet runs locally, it will run properly on your system when you place it on the server. You'll still want to test it, just like you test all of your HTML files.

> **CAUTION**
>
> Users must have Java-capable browsers. If they don't, you should probably use GIF animations or server pushes.

Using the Animation Applet

The applet used here is on your CD. This is what your HTML should look like in order to use it properly:

```
<applet code=Animator.class width=460 height=160>
<param name=imagesource value="images/Beans">
<param name=backgroundcolor value="FFFFFF">
<param name=endimage value=10>
<param name=soundsource value="audio">
<param name=soundtrack value=spacemusic.au>
<param name=sounds value="1.au¦2.au¦3.au¦4.au¦5.au¦6.au¦7.au¦8.au¦
➥9.au¦0.au">
<param name=pause value=200>
</applet>
```

imagesource—the directory set to the location of the images.

backgroundcolor—24-bit hex number used for background.

endimage—the number of images to play. In this case, the first image in the list through the tenth image are played. Image names do not matter for this parameter. There are several other ways to specify which images will play; check out the applets documentation.

soundsource—this sets the URL for the audio files.

sounds—list of audio samples from the directory specified in "soundsource" parameter. This is an URL so it can point to directories other than the one specified in "soundsource."

pause—a pause between frames in milliseconds.

Adjust these parameters and have fun. There are a lot of applets available that you can use and modify as desired. Do check copyright notices. Most files made available for download have a note in the header that frees the creator of any liability and lets you do whatever you want with the code.

Where to Go From Here?

This chapter covered a lot of miscellaneous information about how to make your pages more dynamic. There are other locations in this book where you can find similar content:

- Chapter 12, "All that Shockwave"

  Gives you a look at Macromedia's shockwave and its other multimedia products.

- Chapter 13, "Making the Most of Multimedia"

  Introduces you to a variety of multimedia formats and applications.

- Chapter 14, "Java, Cookies, and other Tricks"

  Shows you how to increase the interest of your pages by incorporating Java, JavaScript, and Cookies.

- Chapter 15, "CGI Scripts"

  Introduces you to the power of CGI scripts with lots of examples and "how-to" informations.

Part
III

Ch
9

Sounds

Putting Audio on Your Web Page

Sooner or later you will want to add audio to a Web site. This chapter gives you key tips on how to get audio, and how to put it on your pages quickly. Since audio files can be very large, you'll find descriptions of new and easy ways to implement technologies for giving end users access to many files, while minimizing the amount of time that it takes to download audio pages. An example of a possible implementation can be seen in Figure 10.1.

Audio files of various formats are only now becoming common on the Web. The lack of audio on the Internet is directly related to the fact that audio is used minimally on computer systems in general; except for "system sounds," your computer is probably mute. If audio was a more intrinsic part of the way people use application programs, then audio would have found its way onto the Web much earlier with a much more defined role.

FIG. 10.1
An audio page
should be con-
structed with controls
so that your clients
have control.

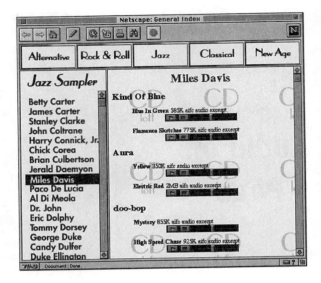

Today, most sound files found on the Web are:

- Audio clips from Web sites that are established to sell music.
- Audio clips designed to be downloaded and used on your computer as "system sounds."
- Sounds from games.
- Sounds from music enthusiasts who collect music.
- MIDI files from musicians who want to share their resources with other enthusiasts.

Microsoft's Internet Explorer and Netscape Navigator support background music in one way or another. Soon the Web will be alive with the sound of music. Implementing audio intelligently will keep people browsing back for more. ■

How and Where to Acquire Audio Content

There are a variety of places you can acquire high-quality audio content. Much of it is labeled "public domain." If it is not public domain, you can frequently get permission from the author to use a sample of his or her music.

Audio Content from the Internet

By using any search engine and key words such as "audio clips," "MIDI files," and "aiff Beatles," you will quickly find many pages with the type of music that you want, already in the proper format. Just because someone's Web site has a folder labeled "public_domain" does not relieve you of the responsibility to make sure the piece of music you are going to use does not fall under copyright protection. If the audio clip you are considering is a sound effect or recording of birds singing, you are probably safe. However, beware of audio clips from *Star Trek* or TV shows that are labeled public domain.

Downloading audio content from Web pages is as easy as downloading images or other content. Audio files can be very large so beware of long download times.

Part
IV

Ch
10

> **CAUTION**
>
> You should get copyright permission before placing content on the Internet. Copyright laws do apply to the Internet. Do not think that using audio clips will go unnoticed. ASCAP has been charging youth camps $500 per year to sing songs like "Happy Birthday" around the campfire; they have actually been enforcing these fees. If you use unauthorized content, you can expect to be the target of copyright litigation in the future (especially if you or your company has some money).

From CDs or DAT Tapes

A wealth of music is available on CD. There are many musicians and music compilation houses that will sell you a CD full of public domain music and sounds—generally for a very reasonable price ($50). In addition, you can "rent audio" on a "needle-drop" basis from some sources. This is common in the television business, where video producers are always looking for background music and jingles for commercials. When you rent audio on a needle-drop basis you are actually buying it per "cut." That is, three 10-second segments will cost you three times more than a single one-minute segment. Pricing scales and practices vary.

Recorded from "Live Sources"

Narration, of course, is something that you can record yourself. Make sure that it meets the quality standards that people throughout your target audience will find acceptable. Creating professional-quality audio is a complicated business. Don't think that by plugging a microphone into the back of your computer you can create a narration that sounds as good as something done in a recording studio, monitored by trained audio technicians. On the other hand, if you are only concerned with annotating an image, this low-quality approach may be completely acceptable to your audience.

Creating Your Own Music

If you are a musician, any of the previous concerns become less important. You can create your own music with old-fashioned analog instruments, then have the music digitized for use on your Web site. Or, you can create and edit your own MIDI files by using computer software, a synthesizer, or a combination of the two. MIDI music files are now playable by most browsers and have many advantages over traditional audio files.

Putting Audio Clips on Your Web Pages

Placing audio clips on your Web pages can be accomplished in one of two ways. You can either include the clip as a selectable hyperlink or you can include the clip as background music that loads and plays by default.

Including the Audio File as a Hyperlink

You can include an audio file as a hyperlink, just like any other type of file. To include audio make sure the audio clip is in a format that can be played by all important browsers. See Chapter 11, "Working With Audio," for more information.

Include the audio clip's name in the <HREF> tag example:

```
<A HREF="openingdoor.aiff">Opening Door Sound Effect</A>
```

Make sure the audio clip loads and plays properly on different platforms and with the versions of browsers that you are targeting.

Optimizing Your Web Site

Place all audio clips on your site in the same audio format (this may not be desirable if you want to share MIDI and other audio clips). Choose the format that you like and stick with it. This will be particularly welcome for visitors who have older browsers that do not support the file types you have on your site. To require users to get one plug-in (or helper application) to listen to content on your site is acceptable. To make them get two or three plug-ins is inconsiderate. If a new format becomes popular, you may want to include the file in two formats (Au and MPEG, for example).

Include as detailed a description as you think is necessary. Again, why is the clip there? With a good description, you may be able to inform the user if this is the file they want, or assure them that the long download will not be worth the wait.

List the file size. Some visitors using a slow modem will not download a 10MB audio file no matter how interesting it may be. See Figure 10.2 for an example of how to label your audio files.

As browsers become more sophisticated, they can handle more and more formats automatically. However, some of your visitors may not have the latest browsers, helper applications, or plug-ins. Because of this, you may want to include references to places where the appropriate plug-ins can be found, or at least a note about the file format.

FIG. 10.2
Always label your
audio content clearly.

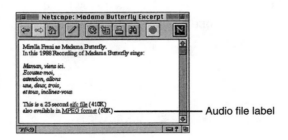

Audio file label

Part
IV

Ch
10

Netscape Navigator and Internet Explorer Extensions

Netscape Navigator and Microsoft's Internet Explorer provide tags that extend and enhance the use of audio on Web pages.

Adding Audio as a Background Sound

Microsoft started the background music phenomenon by introducing the non-standard (enhanced) tag BGSOUND (background sound). This simply points to a sound file that is read and played.

```
<BGSOUND SRC="myvoice.wav">
```

Implementing audio in this way works only for the Internet Explorer browser. There is a more versatile tag, EMBED, that gives you a great deal of flexibility regarding how a background sound is played.

The EMBED tag is supported by most browsers. So, unless there is something that you only want Internet Explorer clients to hear, you should probably use the EMBED tag instead of the BGSOUND tag.

The EMBED tag can be used to play an audio file in the background by including it like this:

```
<EMBED SRC="http://www.my.home/audiofile.aiff" HIDDEN=TRUE
AUTOSTART=TRUE>
```

In the above example, SRC points to the file's URL, the argument HIDDEN=TRUE indicates there will be no controls present, and AUTOSTART=TRUE indicates the audio will start playing in the background as soon as the file is loaded.

> **CAUTION**
>
> Make sure your background audio files are small. Once a client leaves the page bearing the audio file, it stops loading (he won't hear a thing). Don't go through a lot of work creating beautiful background sounds only to have no one hear them.

Adding Controls to Your Audio Files

With Netscape's LiveAudio and Microsoft's ActiveX, you can easily place audio controls on your Web pages. This section is not intended exclusively for programmers, as the steps for placing audio controls on your Web pages are straightforward.

There are several good reasons to add controls to your audio files:

- You let the client know that audio is on the way.
- You give the user volume control.
- You give the user the ability to stop, replay, and pause the audio.

To add an audio control panel to your Web page, use the following tag:

```
<EMBED SRC="URL to audio file" HEIGHT=60 WIDTH=144 CONTROLS=CONSOLE>
```

An actual control panel is implemented like this:

```
<EMBED SRC="symph3.aiff" HEIGHT=60 WIDTH=144 CONTROLS=CONSOLE>
```

This command opens an audio file with a full-size control console, which can be seen in Figure 10.3.

Part
IV

Ch
10

FIG. 10.3
A full-size control console, as it appears on the user's screen.

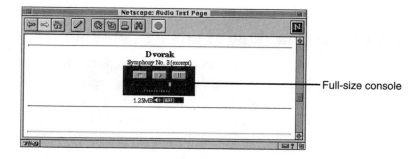

Full-size console

You can also add a smaller control console with the following line:

```
<EMBED SRC="symph9.aiff" HEIGHT=15 WIDTH=144
CONTROLS=SMALLCONSOLE AUTOSTART=TRUE>
```

You will notice that HEIGHT is 15 instead of 60 and that SMALLCONSOLE is specified; this creates the control panel shown in Figure 10.4. In addition, AUTOSTART is set to TRUE, which causes the audio from this clip to load and play at startup.

FIG. 10.4
A smaller control console is created by changing HEIGHT and adding SMALLCONSOLE.

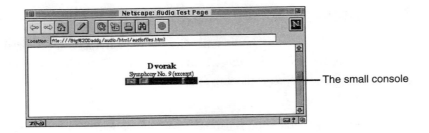

The small console

N O T E Placing an audio control for a background sound is very considerate. It is possible the client does not want to hear the audio clip that you selected. If you do put a series of audio controls on one page, make sure that only one has AUTOSTART=TRUE unless you explicitly want more than one audio clip to play in the background simultaneously. ▣

CAUTION

Each file that is specified with an EMBED command will be downloaded to the client when the Web page is read. This can lead to extreme download times. Please see the next section, "How to Keep Download Times Reasonable," for a solution.

How to Keep Download Times Reasonable

If you follow the previous examples, you can create your own interactive audio Web page. But, each clip may take a significant amount of time to download. So, what happens if you would like to put 25 audio clips on a Web page, each with its own small control console? Download time could be a problem. To work around this difficulty, you can include a JavaScript function that will let you defer the loading of the audio file until the play button is pushed.

This is a simple feature to implement as long as you pay attention to a couple of details.

First, create a file with the OnPlay function calling an audio file. For example:

```
<SCRIPT LANGUAGE=SoundScript>
OnPlay (http://URL/audiofile.mid);
</SCRIPT>
```

Save this script and name it as if it were an audio file (Newworldscript.mid for example).

Then, in your HTML document, include the script's name in place of an audio file's name in the EMBED command. The following is an example of how to do this.

The audio file that you want to play is newworld.mid.

1. Create the three line text file:

```
<SCRIPT LANGUAGE=SoundScript>
OnPlay(newworld.mid);
</SCRIPT>
```

2. Save this file as Newworldscript.mid.

TIP

The name is not important (except for the file's extension). It is just easier to keep track of all of these files if you have a naming convention that you can recognize.

CAUTION

You must use the same extension on this file as the type of file that this script will call. Otherwise, the browser will get ready to play one file type, read a second type, and give you an "Invalid file type" error.

3. In your HTML document, include an EMBED command similar to the ones shown earlier.

```
<EMBED SRC="newworldscript.mid" HEIGHT=15 WIDTH=144
CONTROLS=SMALLCONSOLE>
```

In this example, the audio file's controls will be present, but the actual file will not begin to download until you press the Play button.

Differences between Netscape and Internet Explorer

At the time of this writing, including a single EMBED command that references an audio file will have different effects in Netscape and Internet Explorer. Following is a standard EMBED tag.

```
<EMBED SRC="groovietune.au">
```

Part
IV

Ch

10

Internet Explorer recognizes the file format and provides default audio control for you (see Figure 10.5). In Netscape, nothing appears; Navigator requires that you specify a CONSOLE type; otherwise, no controls will appear. Therefore, make sure to include CONSOLE and a console type. That way, both Netscape Navigator and Internet Explorer clients will have an audio panel.

FIG. 10.5
Internet Explorer
provides a default
audio control for you
when you use the
EMBED tag.

Internet Explorer ignores CONSOLE and SMALLCONSOLE—it recognizes the file type by the extension used and provides a control panel.

Check out Chapter 11, "Working with Audio," for details on audio formats, audio editors, and streaming audio.

Where to Go from Here?

You've just gotten a taste of putting audio on your Web page. There's so much more to do with audio, and it's just so much fun. Check out:

■ Chapter 11, "Working with Audio"

This chapter contains a lot of information about audio. In addition, it has a few quick suggestions on what you can do to edit and modify audio files.

■ The CD-ROM

It contains editing applications that you can spend a week playing with.

■ RealAudio Web site

www.realaudio.com is a great place to go to get the lowdown on cutting edge audio technology.

■ Shockwave Web site

See and hear what Shockwave audio is all about. You can start using the Shockwave stuff without investing in an audio server. Look it over.

## CHAPTER 1

Working with Audio

This chapter is designed to give you valuable information about audio-file formats and audio-editing applications. ■

Audio formats

Audio is available in a variety of formats. Each format has its own particular strengths and weaknesses.

Reducing audio file size

Reasonable file size is a critical concern when putting content on the Web—some suggestions.

Audio editors

There are a lot of tools available as Shareware and Freeware that let you modify your audio quickly and easily.

Streaming audio

Streaming audio lets you listen to the Internet like it is a radio. Without disk space limitations, this is certainly the future of audio on the Internet.

The future of audio

There will be more and more audio options in the future as bandwidth increases and new products become available.

Choosing Appropriate Audio Formats

There are many file formats available to choose from. The first three formats described below (Au, Aiff, Wav) are all very similar in their characteristics and applications. MPEG, MIDI, and MOD, discussed at the end of this section, are interesting because of their differences and the way they represent audio information. As browsers become more powerful, the need for the user to be aware of these different formats becomes less important. It is still critical that you know something about the audio formats so you make the correct choices when putting audio on Web pages.

Au

Au files use μlaw compression; this is a 2:1 compression ratio and is similar in its quality and file size to the Aiff and Wav formats. Au is a format originally employed on NEXT and Sun workstations. It is a very popular format and is supported by most browsers.

Aiff and Aifc

Aiff is a format common on Silicon Graphics UNIX Workstations and Apple Macintosh computer systems. It allows a variety of recording rates and bits. This format is supported by most browsers. Aifc (also referred to as Aiff-c) is a compressed version of Aiff.

Wav

Wav is a format found commonly on the Windows platform. It is supported by most browsers and has file sizes very comparable to Aiff and Au formats.

MPEG

MPEG is a format originally introduced as a video compression algorithm. It is interesting as an audio format because it provides significant compression with a *minimal* loss in audio quality. The process of compressing an audio file for MPEG is called *encoding*. Encoding is processor intensive. Once a file is encoded, it must then be *decoded* on the client side; and again, decoding is processor intensive. The advantage of MPEG is that you can get 8:1 audio compression that sounds very good (most people will never notice the difference between a compressed and uncompressed file), or 16:1 audio compression, which does not sound bad (audiophiles may swoon, but the rest of us may notice that the compressed file sounds slightly hollow or stuffy).

TIP Should you use MPEG? Do you have the tools and the desire to encode audio files (the tools are available as shareware, do you want to encode the files?). Do your clients have machines that are fast enough to decode MPEG files on the fly? Some testing is probably in order. If particular browsers do not support MPEG decoding, many decoders do exist that can be configured as helper applications for the browser.

With the growth of all multimedia content on the Web, you can expect that MPEG players and MPEG support will increase rapidly. After all, an MPEG audio file is simply an MPEG movie file without the video information.

MIDI

MIDI is altogether different from any of the previously discussed audio formats. MIDI contains the "notes" of a song rather than digitized sound. MIDI also indicates which "instruments" should play these notes. The advantage of MIDI is that the file size is very small in comparison to the other formats. The disadvantage is that the MIDI file will sound different depending on which audio samples are included with each system on the client side. For example, Beethoven's Moonlight Serenade may sound like it is playing on a grand piano on your computer, but sound like it is being played on a PlaySkool xylophone on my computer. If you are going to use MIDI files, it is a good idea to hear them on several platforms to make sure you are indeed conveying the appropriate mood. How efficient is MIDI? The entire Moonlight Serenade, which lasts over five minutes, is a 12K MIDI file.

In order for MIDI to sound good, you need good "samples" of the instruments that are specified in the MIDI file. There are relatively inexpensive sound cards for Windows machines that provide extensive MIDI support. On the Macintosh, high-quality MIDI sound is available in software using the QuickTime 2.0 *Musical Instruments* extension.

NOTE MIDI files can be used "outside" of the computer system. Some users will have synthesizers connected to their computer systems, and in other cases, the synthesizers can accept MIDI files on a computer disk. ■

It is not unusual to find archives of MIDI-formatted files that are a megabyte in size and contain hundreds of songs.

Of course there are some obvious limitations to MIDI:

- MIDI does not support speech.
- MIDI does not guarantee clients will hear the same "sound" that you intend them to hear.
- You cannot convert other formats into MIDI.

 TIP If you can find a MIDI sound that you like, you may consider using it as a background sound. MIDI files download very quickly and sound very clear.

Mod

Mod is a format much like MIDI; it is a series of notes and instruments. In addition, Mod files include the samples of the instruments that are being used. Because of this, Mod files are much larger than MIDI files. Mod does guarantee what the audio will sound like. At this time, Mod is not supported as a plug-in for browsers.

Saving Disk Space and Transfer Time

Audio files can be huge. One minute of CD-quality sound will require 10M of disk storage space. Not only are you looking at storage problems at your end, but also unreasonable download times on you client's side. To save significant space, you must throw away some audio information (read quality). There is only one way to determine how much the quality of the audio can be reduced without bothering your audience—by listening to the audio at different rates. In general, audio files are very large. The following chart shows how you can reduce audio file size. All the following files were created in the Aiff format (similar results will occur with μlaw and Wav files). The "Original File" is a 30-second audio file recorded from CD.

	Rate	Channels	Bits	File Size
Original File	44.1kHz	Stereo	16	5,160K
	11.025 kHz	Stereo	16	1,290K
	11.025 kHz	Stereo	8	645K
	11.025 kHz	Mono	8	322K

Which Setting Should You Use?

You must be the judge. Listen to the audio quality and make the following decisions for your audience. Some inexpensive computer audio systems can handle no more than 8kHz mono, eight-bit audio. Who is your client? Are they audiophiles or people looking for chocolate chip cookie recipes? One way around this problem is to include a "low-quality" sample, then let the *very* interested visitor download a higher quality file.

Determining Audio File Size

There is a simple formula that you can use to calculate audio rate:

Bytes/channel * Channels/sample * Samples/sec. = bytes/sec.

Here is an example for CD-quality stereo sound:

2 bytes/channel * 2 channels/sample * 44,100 samples/sec = 176,400 Bps

One second of CD-quality audio requires 172.26K of storage space. A five-minute song requires 50M of storage space. Most of your clients will be viewing these pages with 28.8Kbps modems or less. A good connection with a modem of this type can transfer 1M of data in about five minutes. This results in a transfer time of about four hours for a five minute, CD-quality file. Therefore, you must make some compromises between the audio quality you would like to provide and the amount of time it takes to download that quality. Silicon Graphics provides the following suggestions as a place to start in making your tough quality/file size decisions:

Part

IV

Ch

11

| | | Bits/Bytes per | | |
Contents	Channels	Channel	Rate	Bytes per Sec
Speech	1	8/1	8kHz	8,000bps
Monaural Music	1	8/1	16kHz	16,000bps
Stereo Music	1	8/1	16kHz	16,000bps

Editing Audio Files and Format Conversion

The term *audio editor* covers a wide range of application programs that are used, in some way, to modify audio files. In some cases, they are simply conversion utilities letting you change between file formats. In many cases, audio editors provide a rich set of features for modifying sounds. Effects like echoes, reverbs, and fades can be applied. Others serve as multitrack mixers, as in Figure 11.1.

FIG. 11.1
Sound Sculptor II by Jeff Smith is a very powerful Shareware multitrack, audio-editing application that runs on the Macintosh.

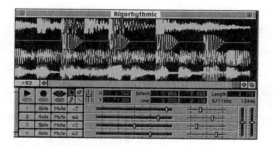

Many of these applications are Shareware or Freeware, meaning you can get a lot of experience editing audio at a very reasonable price. Of course, there are commercial packages available, many of which are part of multimedia packages. After spending some time with these applications, you will be in a very good position to determine exactly what you need for your day-to-day use.

Avoiding that Pop

Each audio card is different. Some of these cards make a "snap" or "pop" when they are either initially powered or, more commonly, when the audio stream ends abruptly, as illustrated in Figure 11.2. You can "fade out" your audio files to help reduce this problem. Most audio-editing applications provide controls that let you perform a number of effects on your audio files. Look at how you can correct this problem.

FIG. 11.2

This audio file may cause a "pop" when your computer finishes playing it. Notice the abrupt end of the audio signal.

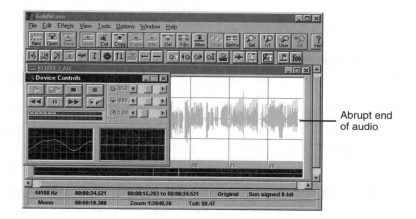

Abrupt end of audio

By making some adjustments in the audio editor you can modify the audio so that it fades out very smoothly, as illustrated in Figure 11.3.

FIG. 11.3

Using Goldwave, by Cris S. Craig, the audio clip has been modified so that it now fades out. With this simple modification the "pop" will be greatly reduced or eliminated.

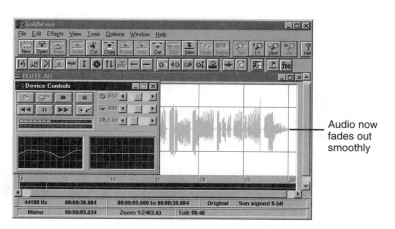

Audio now fades out smoothly

Part

IV

Ch

11

Considering Real-Time "Streaming" Audio

The process of playing audio or video over a network in real time is referred to as *streaming*. With a fast network and a dedicated server, streaming is not a problem. However, when network traffic is variable or network speed is slow, streaming becomes a tremendous challenge.

Why Is Streaming Audio Important

Streaming audio is being used in many ways. It is possible to net-cast live events like concerts and speeches. If you could distort time slightly, you could be a "Net Dead Head," traveling from San Francisco to Chicago to New Orleans, without ever leaving your livingroom.

Being able to transmit audio live provides a tremendous diversity of content: every radio station in the country; street sounds from your favorite corner in New Orleans; every key note address at every industry meeting. All of them live.

Another advantage of streaming has nothing to do with the "live" part of the equation. Let's assume that you are doing research on Bill Clinton's speeches and their topics according to region. You could go to the President Clinton virtual museum (if one exists) and listen to all of his speeches. That would be possible today with nonstreaming audio, but consider the problems. You must first download very large audio files to your hard disk drive, then play and listen to them, and, because of space constraints, delete them—only to find one week later that you need the information from the August 26th speech that you just deleted from your disk. With a library built upon streaming data, you simply connect to the virtual museum, find the file that you are looking for, then play it. When you have heard enough, you can stop it; if you want to replay part of the speech, you can rewind it; or, you can fast forward to the section and topic that you want to listen to. A good museum would provide hyperlinks to different parts of the audio by topic and keyword.

Streaming audio changes the way you think about and use audio. Storage and transmission time, your two biggest problems, have been solved.

RealAudio

RealAudio is the pioneer in popularizing audio streaming over the Internet. Using RealAudio, you can encode a one-minute-long 2.6M .Wav or an .Au file can be reduced to either a 60K audio file, designed to be streamed over a 14.4Kbps connection, or a 113K audio file, designed to be streamed over a 28.8Kbps connection. There is no way that any compression scheme can get this magnitude of compression without sacrificing significant audio information. However, in the case of the 60K file, you can clearly hear a speaker's voice and, with the 113K file, you can hear mono music that sounds like a good AM radio station. RealAudio accomplishes the compression by throwing out a lot of information contained in the original audio clip. For example, the 60K files are optimized for the dynamic range of the human voice; dynamic range is intentionally limited so that the "important" audio information is not discarded.

In addition to encoding, RealAudio uses a different network protocol. RealAudio can use TCP (Transmission Control Protocol), but in most cases uses UDP (User Datagramm Protocol). While TCP assures complete transmission of data (the emphasis is on data integrity), it is rather poor at maintaining a constant rate of transmission (critical if you are trying to listen to audio). UDP, on the other hand, looses data frequently, but is much better than TCP at maintaining a constant rate. For streamed audio, this constant rate is more important than an occasional "drop out." Heavy network traffic will wreak havoc on any streamed data—you need a RealAudio server. You cannot just place files in RealAudio format on your site and have them stream in real time.

Part
IV

Ch
11

Macromedia's Shockwave

Shockwave is more than streamed audio. It is actually designed as a solution for delivering multimedia content over the network. Macromedia's Director product is wildly popular for creating and organizing multimedia presentations. It is only natural that streaming audio should be part of that solution. Shockwave provides compression rates that allow audio streaming. Shockwave operates using TCP, so audio is transmitted completely. In order to combat some of the drop outs that you would invariably encounter by using a TCP connection, Shockwave has incorporated features that let you specify how much of the audio file you want to download before the audio starts playing. That is, Shockwave creates an audio buffer protecting itself from network delays. Shockwave does not require special server software; however, it does require the purchase of the authoring software.

Which Product Is Better?

At the time of this writing, RealAudio is the more mature product and provides a greater feature set than does Shockwave (for example, the ability to pause, rewind, and do live broadcasts). RealAudio does require a special server. If you do not have access to a RealAudio server, you will have to find one that you can use (at least for your audio links). Shockwave does not require a special server. Both products require software purchases. If you are serious about putting together a site with lots of audio content, you should carefully evaluate these, as well as other streaming audio products that may appear in the market. Preparing this type of content is a considerable time investment, and you certainly want to make the best decision for your clients and your business model. Both RealAudio and Macromedia are constantly improving their products. For example, RealAudio has just added stereo support. So check around and see what is new. Some of these new features make dramatic improvements to your listening experience.

To get started using Real Audio, you need to invest almost $800 into providing a server that five people can access simultaneously. Providing a server that can stream up to 100 simultaneous users will cost over $11,000. There are also hardware concerns. You need a tremendously wide connection for your server once you start streaming audio. Please check the appropriate specifications at **www.realaudio.com**.

What Is the Future of Audio on the Internet?

You can expect that all common (and even some uncommon) audio formats will be supported by browsers in the future. This is a very competitive industry. Supporting additional audio formats is fairly easy and gives the browser companies something to talk about. As transmission moves from phone lines to cable, satellite, and other high-bandwidth technologies, the size and format of audio files will become less important.

Where to Go From Here?

This chapter contained information about audio formats and a little bit about audio editors. You can have fun with audio, so check out the following:

- Chapter 10, "Putting Audio on Your Web Page"

  This chapter contains good information about exactly how to place audio on your pages.

- Go to MIDI Sites

  There are many wonderful MIDI sites on the Internet. Make sure you seek them out.

- See What the Record Companies Are Doing

  It's their business. But, because of the inherently low bandwidth of the average consumer's connection to the internet, the audio files are either high quality and huge, or are of low quality and small file size.

- See RealAudio and ShockWave

  These are the best two current technologies. Check them out and see which one might work for you.

Part
IV

Ch
11

Multimedia

## CHAPTER 12

All that Shockwave

Macromedia has produced desktop multimedia applications for years. Its focus has been to provide users with tools that they can use to create presentations, usually rather small in size, that are capable of playback on computer systems. Over the years, these capabilities have grown to include medium-quality audio, video, 3D graphics, 2D design and other elements. Macromedia's foray into the Internet was a logical choice. That is, to provide the same type of content for presentations and interactive sessions to users across the Internet.

Macromedia's approach to the Internet is most directly seen by its development of the "Shockwave" plug-ins. These plug-ins, which can be added to Netscape Navigator and Microsoft Internet Explorer, let users view Macromedia-produced audio and multimedia content from within the familiar surroundings of a browser. Content produced for Shockwave viewing is compressed specifically for the low-bandwidth reality of most Internet connections. The capability

Shockwave plug-ins

Macromedia has developed plug-ins for Web browsers that support specially compressed audio and multimedia content.

Multimedia presentations

Macromedia Director is the most popular multimedia creation and editing tool in the world.

Image processing, effects, and manipulation

Macromedia xRes is a product designed to compete with Photoshop's compositing, image processing, and high-resolution image manipulation.

Professional-quality illustration

FreeHand is a professional-level, vector-based illustration package.

3D modeling and animation

Extreme 3D provides tools for creating three-dimensional models, including VRML worlds.

Audio editing and production

Both traditional, high-quality audio and audio optimized for playback via Shockwave are available.

of browsers to accept plug-ins is a key architectural element that provides a method for Macromedia to distribute standard player and display technologies.

It's strange how standards get set on Internet-related issues. Sometimes, they occur through standards committees like W3C, sometimes by companies throwing programming languages or other technologies into the public domain. Macromedia has its own approach to this process. Because Macromedia's products are so diverse and support a number of standards already, its primary concern is distributing players that can handle each of these formats for browsers via plug-ins. The whole Shockwave technology is designed around producing multimedia content of a known compressed format and, at the same time, providing plug-ins to make the viewing of that content possible. Shockwave's audio format is a very popular technology for letting listeners preview CDs, as shown in Figure 12.1. ■

FIG. 12.1
The Macromedia Shockwave experience can be artistic, professional, informative, or just fun.

Putting Macromedia Content on Your Web Page

Director movies and other types of Macromedia content can be put on your Web pages by using the EMBED tag. If users have the correct Shockwave plug-in installed, the content will be accessible in the browser window.

Use the EMBED tag as:

```
<EMBED SRC="path/filename.ext" WIDTH=width HEIGHT=height
PALETTE=ground BGCOLOR=color PLUGINSPAGE="url">
```

Where:

SRC="path/filename.ext" specifies the URL of the content.

WIDTH is the width of the content in pixels.

HEIGHT is the height of the content in pixels.

N O T E Browsers will crop the movie to fit in the viewport that you have specified. ■

PALETTE=ground can be set to "foreground" or "background"

When PALETTE=foreground:

The Director movie's palette is loaded and is used as the palette for the entire page. This can affect the appearance of other graphics on the page.

When PALETTE=background:

The system's palette is loaded for the movie. This is the default when the movie is loaded via the EMBED tag.

BGCOLOR=color specifies the color specified behind the movie.

PLUGINSPACE=URL, this should be set to:

```
PLUGINSPAGE="http://www.macromedia.com/shockwave"
```

An Example

The following command opens a window for a shocked Director movie, as can be seen in Figure 12.2. In this case, the movie's size is 250×200; however, you want to include a 20-pixel, black border around the edge of the movie. Director's color palette will be used in this example.

```
<EMBED SRC="path_to_movie/movie.dcr" BGCOLOR="black" WIDTH=290
HEIGHT=240 PALETTE=foreground>
```

N O T E Remember, you can also use the <NOEMBED> tag to specify content that will be displayed in cases where the shockwave content cannot be used by the browser. ■

FIG. 12.2

A director movie placed in an HTML document by using the EMBED command. Here the director movie vibrates when the pointer is moved over it.

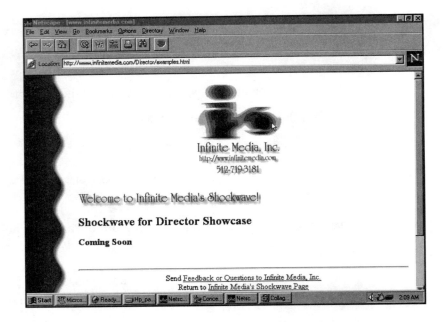

Worry About Bandwidth and Movie Size

Yes, isn't it always a matter of bandwidth? Nothing will kill a viewer's interest more quickly than making them wait too long for content to download. I'm afraid that's an issue you'll be struggling with for quite some time.

Some general suggestions:

■ Use afterburner to compress movies.

Afterburner is the utility that lets you compress movies and make them Shockwave ready. Use this utility! It's the most important, single thing you can do.

- Keep movies small.

  Don't count on compression to solve your problems. When developing content for the Internet, keep clips short and small in size. You cannot depend on having tremendous bandwidth. If you have some beautiful high-resolution content that must be shown to end users, you should find a different medium like Photo CD, CD-ROM, or videotape.

- Consider the content type.

  People will wait longer to download content that can be interacted with. For example, I'll wait a while for a game that I can use over and over. It is doubtful that I'd be as interested in downloading a long movie file that I'll lose interest in after one viewing.

- Use eight-bit graphics.

  You can refer to Chapter 5, "Cool Effects with Images," for more information about color optimization. Here, color depth is important to consider as a design criterion early on. If you know your content will be distributed over the Internet, stick with eight-bit (256) color images. Download time will be less than graphics with higher color resolution, and some low-end systems may not support something greater than 256 colors.

- Change other Director elements to eight bits.

  There are methods for reducing cast members to lower color resolution. You should check the Macromedia Director documentation. There is also a list of palette concerns that you may want to investigate, depending on the platform on which the movie was created and the color palettes selected while creating the movie.

Part
V

Ch
12

Macromedia Product Overviews

Macromedia has an entire group of products that provide unique solutions to the Desktop graphic designer and multimedia creator. This section gives a thumbnail sketch of each of these applications.

Director

Director is the multimedia authoring tool that has made Macromedia famous; you can get a quick view of its interface in Figure 12.3. Director is used for creating interactive presentations for kiosks, CD-ROM titles, and simulations. Now, Director content is finding its way onto the Internet. The output from Director is normally referred to as a movie, even though there may be nothing particularly movie-like about the production.

FIG. 12.3
Director provides a tool-rich environment for assembling multimedia content.

Director can also export files as QuickTime movies. You might want to consider providing your content in two formats when it makes sense—as a Director movie and a QuickTime movie.

FreeHand Graphics Design Studio

The FreeHand Graphics Design Studio contains the popular drawing package FreeHand, Macromedia xRes, Extreme 3D, and Fontographer. These products are available separately or can be purchased in this design-studio configuration. A key feature of each of these products is that their content can be optimized then put on the Web and accessed with the Shockwave plug-in.

Freehand   FreeHand is an illustration package. The vector files that it creates and supports let users zoom in to very high resolutions. These resolutions are only limited by your desire to add detail. The map in Figure 12.4 can be zoomed way in with all graphic elements maintaining their integrity.

FIG. 12.4
Vector graphics can be zoomed to a great degree and still look good.

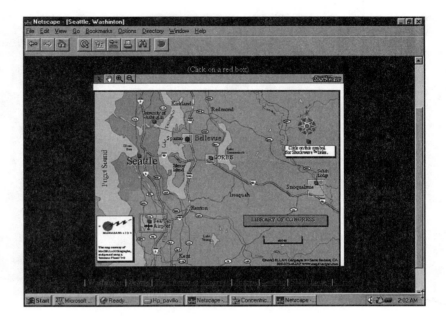

xRES   xRes is a special effects and compositing tool. This tool supports progressive JPEG, GIF and many other formats. Different painting techniques can be simulated. Want a photograph transformed into something that looks like a Monet? This application can do it for you. xRes provides 32 layers for compositing. In addition, it runs in two modes; one mode handles small images quickly and easily, and the xRes mode lets you work at surprising speeds with images of high resolutions.

Extreme 3D   Extreme 3D is targeted directly at the VRML segment of the Internet clan. Extreme 3D uses a spline-based modeling tool. Object surfaces can be modified using vertex-based editing functions. Deformations are supported. Of interest to you, 3D extreme has controls that let you interactively reduce the number of polygons that make up a surface (critical for keeping database size under control). Extreme 3D supports VRML 1 & 2, so file format compatibility is assured. In addition, you can actually assign URLs to individual objects. When users click objects in these virtual spaces, they will be moved to new worlds (or old worlds depending on where you send them). Exteme 3D's interface can be seen in Figure 12.5.

FIG. 12.5
Wire frame and rendered modes give you flexibility, depending on the complexity of your scene.

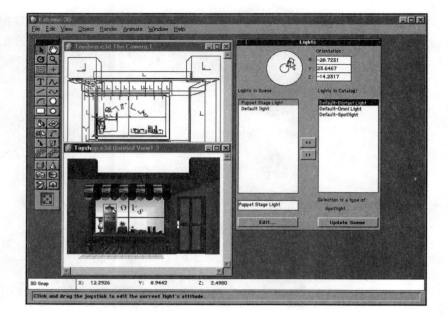

Fontographer   Fontographer is a package that lets you create custom fonts and modify existing faces. Features include the ability to add fractions and logos, create heavier or lighter versions of faces, and adjust spacing and kerning. You can even scan logos and signatures, autotrace them, and convert them into fonts.

SoundEdit 16, Deck II, and Sonic Sound Forge

These are a series of tools designed to create and edit high-quality audio tracks. File formats supported include WAV, MOV, and AIFF. With DECK II, sounds can be recorded to disk in real time. Sonic sound forge lets you create special effects and edit audio one channel at a time.

It's All There

Macromedia does present a pretty strong argument for providing the most complete multimedia authoring tools. These tools are reasonably priced and can provide your site with some much needed sex appeal. There are demonstration versions of some of these products on the CD.

If you ever have a chance to break away from being a Web master for a while, you should look at these multimedia products. Some of them offer very interesting interactive capabilities.

Where to Go from Here?

Macromedia's products are well known and easy to use. There are other ways to add interesting content to your pages described elsewhere in this book. You might want to check out:

- **www.macromedia.com**

    This is Macromedia's Web site and contains all the latest information on Shockwave and the associated products.

- Chapter 11, "Working with Audio"

    See this chapter for audio considerations to Shockwave and to alternate audio formats.

- **WWW.REALAUDIO.COM**

    This is Macromedia's biggest competition for good audio on the Internet.

- Chapter 13, "Making the Most of Multimedia"

    Multimedia is available outside the Macromedia umbrella; look here for some information.

Part
V

Ch
12

Making the Most of Multimedia

Multimedia on the Internet is much more than movies with soundtracks. It now includes Virtual Reality as well. If you haven't looked at any of the Virtual Reality sites, you should do so now. You can try **www.planet9.com**, **vrml.sgi.com**, or **www.paragraph.com**. Although it is a technology that requires a specific set of tools and a good deal of time to master, it is sure to be an important technology for the future. ■

QuickTime movies

QuickTime is an Apple-developed technology that adds audio and video to Web pages. Its flexibility provides solutions for many formats.

QuickTime VR technology

QuickTime VR is a Virtual Reality technology that works particularly well for presenting real-life scenes and objects to online viewers.

VRML, Virtual Reality Modeling Language

VRML is a language designed to place 3D models on the Internet. This technology provides a powerful method for creating new worlds and simulating current ones.

Apple QuickTime

QuickTime is a standard movie format for moving content around the computer world. QuickTime is such a standard that it is used and supported by practically all multimedia applications running on all platforms. This is true of shareware products that cost $100 to sophisticated, professional broadcast editing systems costing tens of thousands of dollars. In this section, you will concentrate on issues that you encounter while putting content on your Web pages.

Putting QuickTime on Your Web Page

Placing a QuickTime movie on your Web page is as easy as putting an image on your page, and will look like the movie in Figure 13.1. You will use the <EMBED> tag. You have a QuickTime movie named "quickpix.mov". "quickpix.mov" has a resolution of 150 vertical pixels and 200 horizontal pixels. Use the following tag:

```
<EMBED SRC="SampleQT.mov" HEIGHT=174 WIDTH=200>
```

Notice how the HEIGHT and WIDTH are used. By default a 24-pixel controller is placed beneath the movie so that you can pause, stop, and start the movie. This controller requires 24 pixels, so 150 pixels plus 24 pixels equals 174 pixels, which is the number used in the preceding example. If you decide to set "controller=false" as part of the EMBED tag, do not add these 24 extra pixels.

NOTE If you don't know the dimensions of the movie, open it with the Movie Player and check its size. Also, it's a good idea to always list the approximate size of the movie in "K" or "MB," so users can decide if they want to wait for the download, or download the movie in the background. ■

QuickTime's Fast-Start Option

As distribution over the Internet has become a more important concern, so has the necessity to let people start to see video and audio while it is downloading. People dont enjoy waiting for an entire movie to download only to discover it was the wrong clip after all.

QuickTime now has a Quick Start option, which is supported in the newest QuickTime MoviePlayer and plug-ins (version 2.5 or later).

FIG. 13.1

A common site on the Internet—a QuickTime movie; hmmm... is it too long to download?

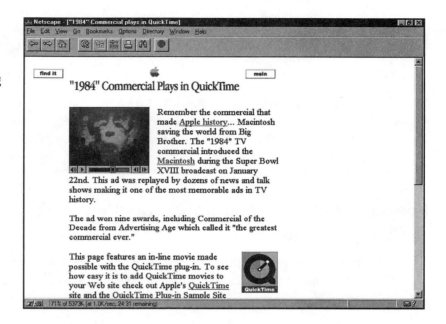

When you use Movie Player, to make movies "Web ready" you should make sure that you:

■ Get the latest MoviePlayer.

The MoviePlayer is always being optimized. Internet applications have become very critical to Apple, so it is a good guess that options will be continually added to MoviePlayer for Internet publishing. The older QuickTime format stored important information about the movie at the end of the movie file. Therefore, it was not possible to begin playing the movie until the entire movie had downloaded. In the new format this information has been moved to the front of the file, allowing for early download and "fast-start" playing.

■ Save the movie as "self contained" and "playable on other computers."

When you are saving the movie from MoviePlayer or QuickTime generating applications, it is critical that you select the "self contained" and "playable on other computers" options. There is a basic difference between the way files are stored on the Macintosh and on other systems. The Macintosh actually stores what would be the "header" information of a DOS file in a separate file.

Part
V

Ch
13

By selecting the two previously mentioned options, you can assure the file type will appear in a format that is recognizable and usable on DOS, Windows, UNIX, and Macintosh systems.

 T I P There is a tool that Apple now provides named the *Internet Movie Tool;* you can acquire it from the Apple QuickTime page. Not only does the Internet Movie Tool let you save movies as "fast-start," it also lets you batch convert movies. So, if you have a lot of movies to convert, this is a very helpful utility.

Considerations for Internet Distribution of QuickTime Movies

QuickTime has been such a popular format for Digital Video and CD-ROM productions that two points should be remembered when putting QuickTime movies on Web pages:

- Movies are large; download times can be outrageous.

    It is common for a 20-second QuickTime movie to be several megabytes in size. This is fine for CD-ROM delivery. However, if your customers are connected via 28.8 modems or less, the download times will probably be unacceptable, considering the type of information you want to present. Even over a fast connection download time can be considerable.

- Reduce file size.

    Make the movies as small as possible. If the content is good, video quality and size can suffer and the output will still be entertaining. Use a tool like Movie Cleaner, available from Terran Interactive (**http://terran-int.com/**), which has preprocessing features that make movies look good at low-data rates.

- Create links to large movie files.

    Don't start downloading large movies automatically. Place a link on the page that users can click if they want to view the movie. Be creative here; either use a representative frame from the movie as a button, or create a little GIF animation labelled with text that reads something like: "this is a sample of the QuickTime movie 'Nerd World Three' click on the animation to download the 250MB file."

QuickTime Attributes

There are a series of attributes that can be used within the EMBED tag to affect the appearance and behavior of the movie. Again, a typical EMBED tag specifying a QuickTime movie looks like this:

```
<EMBED SRC=mymovie.mov HEIGHT=99 WIDTH=100>
```

The following is a very brief synopsis. Please see **http://www.apple.com** for more detailed information.

SRC=url—This is the URL of the movie that you want to play.

PLUGINSPAGE=url—If you want to be a Web master's Web master, this is an attribute that you should use. PlugInsPage lets you specify the URL for the QuickTime plug-in if it is not found. If Netscape cannot find the plug-in, it will warn the user and let the user bring up the URL where the QuickTime plug-in can be found. Set this parameter to **http://quicktime.apple.com**. This option is useful for both QuickTime movies and QuickTime VR Objects and Panoramas.

WIDTH=size—The movie's width in pixels.

HEIGHT=size—The movie's height in pixels. Remember to add 24 pixels to the height to allow room for the controls, unless you explicitly set the controller to FALSE.

HIDDEN—This parameter hides the movie. I guess it only makes sense if you want to play an audio-only movie with no controls.

AUTOPLAY=value—When AUTOPLAY=TRUE the movie begins playing as soon as the QuickTime plug-in calculates the rest of the movie will download before the movie reaches the end. Of course, this cannot be guaranteed, depending on your connection. AUTOPLAY=FALSE is the default.

CONTROLLER=value—When CONTROLLER=FALSE is specified the controller does not appear. The user then has control of the movie when clicking over the movie. CONTROLLER=TRUE is the default.

LOOP=value—Values are FALSE (the default) and TRUE (movie loops until it is stopped). PALINDROME plays the movie forward then backward until it is stopped.

Part

V

Ch

13

PLAYEVERYFRAME=value—PLAYEVERYFRAME=TRUE guarantees that every frame of the movie will be played, regardless of how slowly the movie plays. PLAYEVERYFRAME=TRUE turns audio off, because an audio play rate cannot be guaranteed.

HREF=url—As always, HREF links to an URL.

TARGET=frame—Used with the HREF tag and supports any valid target names. See Chapter 4, "Using Frames Effectively," for more information.

QuickTime's Flexibility

One of the nice things about QuickTime is it supports so many formats. These include movie files, QuickTime Virtual Reality files, and MIDI music files.

- To convert a MIDI file to QuickTime simply open the file in movie converter and save it as a movie file.
- Create animations and save them as QuickTime movies.
- QuickTime Virtual Reality files (covered later in this chapter) add, literally, a whole new dimension to your Web pages.

QuickTime VR Is Virtually Amazing

QuickTime VR is a new technology that provides extremely compelling content. QuickTime VR can be used to put 3D, computer-rendered scenes and objects on Web pages, and it can also be used for creating photographic panoramas of real locations and real objects that one can explore. Download time is reasonable, and the interactivity on even a relatively modest computer system is somewhat astounding. You do need the QuickTime QTVR plug-in to view this content.

There are three types of QTVR movies:

- An Object

  An Object is an interactive element that can be viewed continuously throughout 360 degrees of rotation. Figure 13.2 shows an automobile that is a QTVR object. You can spin this car around, look at its trunk, its profile, and the front of the car. In some cases, objects can be spun around so they can be viewed from the top and bottom as well.

■ A Panorama

A Panorama is a scene that can be viewed in all directions. In a panorama the viewpoint is stationary at a position called a "node," but the viewpoint can be changed, letting you look wherever you want. A Panorama is like standing outside in one location and turning around. You can look up, down, left, and right but you cannot move. Figure13.3 shows a good example of a panorama.

■ A Scene

A Scene is made up of multiple nodes and can include objects. You can jump from node to node and click objects to examine them. If the nodes are spaced properly, you can get a sense of continual motion from one location to another.

FIG. 13.2
You can spin this car around interactively. It's the only way I'll ever be able to touch one.

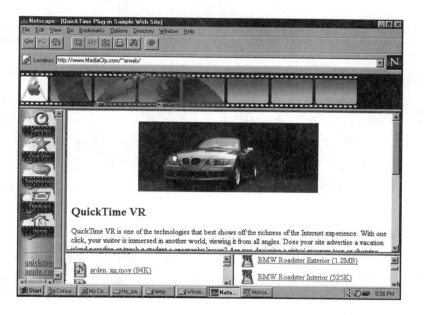

There is a problem with this technology (one that it shares with VRML). The problem is that content creation is time-consuming and can be very expensive. Putting this content on your page is a snap. The only problem is obtaining it!

FIG. 13.3
In this example, you can pan around the scene. It's almost like being there. You can look left, right, up, and down. Even when a QTVR image takes up a small portion of the screen, the effect is impressive.

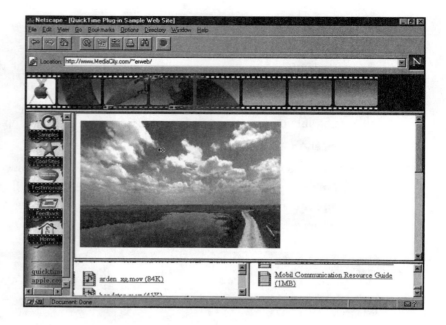

Plopping the QTVR on Your Page

Placing the QuickTime VR image on your page is just as easy as putting any other element into an HTML document. The following line works.

```
<EMBED SRC="pan.mov" HEIGHT=172 WIDTH=402 CONTROLLER=FALSE LOOP=FALSE>
```

QTVR—An Enabling Technology

QuickTime VR is so powerful because it lets you visit places that you have never been before. It also lets you construct worlds, real or imagined, where your user could not afford to go or could not go because of physical constraints.

There are currently significant barriers present for those wanting to get involved in this technology. You need the QuickTime Authoring Suite, which lets you create images in the proper format and provides very in-depth instruction and great sample materials. For example, the kit comes with a video tape that leads you through the process of creating a QTVR scene by using traditional photography; registration, lighting planning, and so on are extremely critical. You just don't take your Sure Shot to the edge of the Grand Canyon and expect to come back with some pictures that you can turn into a really cool panorama.

N O T E Even though this technology isn't extremely cheap or easy, the tools are available for the professional or dedicated amateur to do a nice job of creating content. At this point, this technology does fall more into the realm of the professional photographer or graphic artist than it does the Web master looking for a whiz bang effect. Unless, of course, you have a source for the content. ■

Fun with VRML

VRML, pronounced *vermil*, is the Virtual Reality Modeling Language. If you've had any experience with 3D computer graphic applications, most of the concepts here should seem pretty straightforward. If you haven't, don't panic. You will find software and examples on the accompanying CD to play with when you have a chance.

FIG. 13.4
ParaGraph has a virtual office—quite appropriate for a virtual-reality company. Do they really need desks? Notice that 3D objects can have links to other URLs.

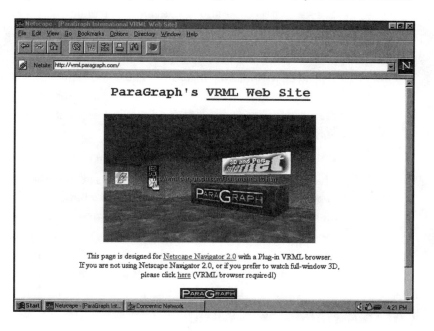

Part
V

Ch
13

It is the intention of the VRML specification to create an environment where virtual 3D worlds can interact across the Internet. This is much more than creating pretty pictures. It holds tremendous possibilities for scientists, architects, mathematicians, and latter-day virtual explorers.

There are at least three ways you see VRML implemented:

■ Simulations of real-world places

This is the easiest thing for us to understand. You go to San Francisco, look around, go to an art gallery, walk inside, see something you like, and buy it. Even today this could be much more than a toy if scenes were constructed more accurately. Say you've never been to the Palace at Auburn Hills, and you're flying into Detroit next week to catch a basketball game. You should be able to sit in front of your computer and drive from Metro airport to the palace. If there is a really long boring stretch of highway, you can click the next off ramp and kind of "hyperspace" to the location. By doing this first on your computer, you not only had a little bit of fun, but you can feel much more comfortable with where you're going. You know which lane you should be in. You know that past the Calvin Klein billboard you take the exit. Strange cities won't seem as strange anymore. Virtual Reality will make the real world safer.

■ Creation of virtual worlds similar to ours

This even includes alien colonies and so on. The idea is you are basically traveling around artificial environments and interacting with other beings in this space. These can be other virtual travelers like yourself or computer-generated beings, angels, or devils.

■ Creations and simulation of virtual systems

This can really be anything else—systems visual or invisible, with different degrees of interactivity. The beautiful thing here is that two people working on similar tasks can create interactive mathematical or physical systems, then see how they react with each other. These can be models of psychologies, models of physical structures, or virtually any models that you can imagine with the Internet as the central nervous system.

Get Your Hands on a World

3D modeling falls outside the scope of this book. But, that doesn't mean you cannot add VRML to your Web pages. Other people have gone to the trouble of building objects that you can download and use. Of course, as always, make sure you get permission. In this case, download a room like the one in Figure 3.5. This room was downloaded from ParaGraph. The file with all the textures and other elements needed to modify this model was contained in a ".MUS" file.

FIG. 13.5
The original file as it appears on ParaGraph's Web site.

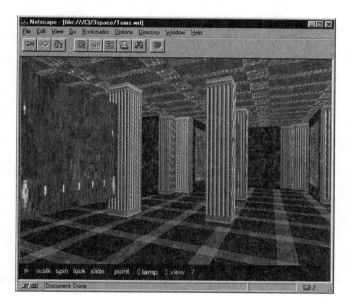

Color Your World

Now open up this world in Virtual Home Space Builder. This application is a Virtual Reality editing application and can be seen in Figure 13.6. You can add objects, move your camera position, set up motion paths, and change lighting and textures, all in this program. It's really quite intuitive.

So, now open the file named steel.mus. This file contains everything necessary to create the look of this scene. Before making any modifications, save it to a file name that you will remember.

In this case, you are only changing the textures on the walls and ceilings. If you click objects, you can see which texture is assigned to each object (notice that they are all ".bmp" files).

Part
V

Ch
13

Open your favorite paint program. Find the ".bmp" files that you want to modify. They are probably in the same file as the steel.mus file. Open these images and notice their resolution and appearance.

FIG. 13.6
Virtual Home Space Builder provides an easy-to-use environment. Start out by changing simple things like the textures on the walls.

The scene preview window

The airbrush window is used to modify texture maps

The builder window for modeling

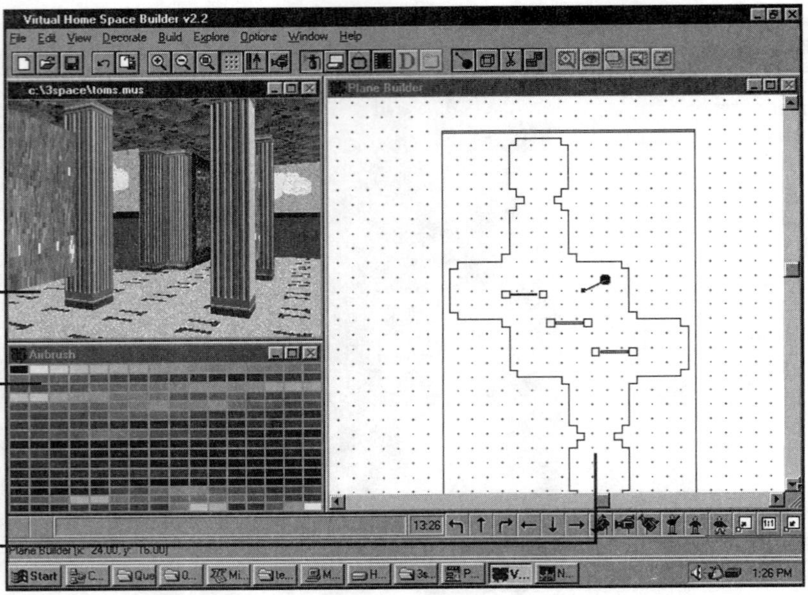

At this point, you can either modify these texture maps or replace them by saving the images that you want to use over their names.

Now reopen your ".MUS" file. Notice how the appearance has changed. In this case, the walls, ceiling, and floors have been changed. It's redecorating the easy way, as you can see in Figure 13.7.

Save this file as a ".wrl" file.

N O T E ".wrl" is the extension applied to VRML worlds. ■

Putting Your World on Your Page

Now, for the fun part. You can make your world visible to your viewers in one of two ways.

FIG. 13.7
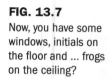
Now, you have some windows, initials on the floor and ... frogs on the ceiling?

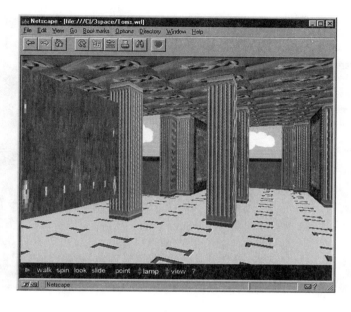

- You can link to your WRL file

  When you link to a WRL file, your browser fills up with the Virtual World.
- You can EMBED your WRL file

  When you EMBED the WRL file, it appears on your page.

Linking to a WRL is the standard method of accessing a WRL. Using this method, your browser fills with the image, and you have controls along the bottom of the screen. Use the following line:

```
<A HREF="URL_myworld.wrl">link</A>
```

It's just a standard link, exactly as if you were referencing any other HTML document. Your browser will appear as in Figure 13.8.

EMBED a WRL in your document when you want it to appear as a portal through your page, as in Figure 13.9. Maybe you have a lot to say about the world that you're looking at. There's no better place to do it than on the same page. EMBED works great when you're placing an object on the page that you are going to just spin around. You can use EMBED like this:

```
<EMBED SRC="URL_myworld.wrl" HEIGHT=240 WIDTH=320>
```

Part
V
Ch
13

FIG. 13.8
The browser has controls along the bottom of the screen, and the VRML environment takes up the entire browser window when you link directly to a WRL.

FIG. 13.9
This is an example of an embedded page. Just wanted to make sure that you didn't get lost out there in space.

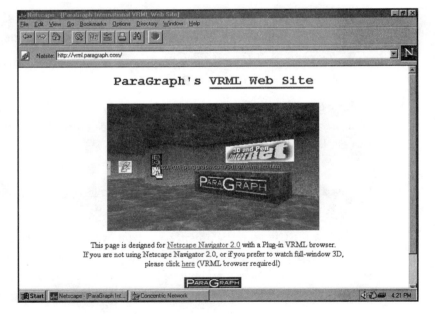

Get Plugged In

Netscape's Live3D plug-in works very nicely for viewing most worlds. Another plug-in that you may want to try is the Cosmo Player plug-in, available from Silicon Graphics Incorporated. This plug-in is available on the CD. SGI has been the leader in 3D computer graphics for a decade. It brings a great deal of expertise to this arena. You should check out its site for some very extravagant content.

Where to Go from Here?

VRML is a technology you can only get familiar with by diving in and exploring it. It's approachable if you pick out a reasonable project for your first experience. For more information on VRML and QTVR:

- ■ The CD-ROM.
  Look at Home Space Builder.
- ■ **www.apple.com**.
  Find out more about QTVR.
- ■ **vrml.sgi.com** and **www.planet9.com**.
  For some great examples of VRML content.
- ■ **www.paragraph.com** and **www.viewpoint.com**.
  For models you can download.

Part
V

Ch
13

Behind the Scenes

## CHAPTER 14

Java, Cookies, and Other Tricks

This chapter is mostly about Java, the programming language that is revolutionizing the way applications are written and distributed. With Java, your browser can be turned into a word processor, an image viewer, a paint application, or just about anything else that you can think of. Java is still relatively new, so the samples used here are pretty simple. At the end of this chapter, you cover two other topics. One is about opening another browser window from a link, the other is a brief discussion about "cookies"—yes, they are a treat.

Changing the way your browser functions has so far been accomplished by installing plug-ins and assigning helper types. But, what if it were possible to download very small, efficient applications that were especially designed for the type of data that you were accessing. You wouldn't have to configure it, install it, or delete it when you were done. It simply worked. This is the capability that Java brings to the Internet today. ∎

What Is Java anyway?

Java is a compiled, portable, and very compact programming language that is multithreaded and runs on nearly all computing platforms. It's going to be huge, so introduce yourself.

How to use applets

Put a Java applet on your page. Test it. Modify it. Put it on your server.

The Java programming language

If you are a programmer, all the tools that you need are provided in the Java Developers Kit (JDK) on the CD.

JavaScript, what it is

Here you will put some JavaScript on a page, and modify it enough so that you understand how it works.

What's a "cookie"

Persistent Client State HTTP Cookies let you place information into visitors' browsers, so you can track where they've gone and what they've done.

What's the Buzz about Java?

Java is a compiled programming language that runs wonderfully across the Internet on multiple platforms. The ability to run Java applets (small applications) is included in almost all browsers. Java solves many problems for many people and could be used for the following:

- Getting software updates automatically

  When you download data that uses an applet, the applet is downloaded each time. This means that, if you change the applet, the new code downloads the next time a user accesses the data. This lets developers start out with simple applets that get the job done and then improve them over time as customer's needs and desires change.

- Running Java on all platforms

  It has been a tremendous hurdle for developers to create different versions of their programs that run on Macintosh, Windows, and UNIX workstations.

- Developing small programs

  For anything to be useful over the Internet, it had better be small. Java is a very compact programming language.

- Incorporating multimedia quickly

  The Java language itself includes classes specifically designed to handle audio and graphics. This gives the developer tools to quickly incorporate these elements without developing a bunch of code that is only designed to support this type of data.

Gulping Full-Strength Java and Applets

You can place applets on your pages just like you can almost any other elements in HTML. Even though you will do no programming here, the applets that are provided on the CD contain a series of parameters that you can modify. These parameters give you control over how the applet behaves. Of course, the number of parameters and their effectiveness are completely dependent upon what the applet programmer decided was important, expedient, or both.

Placing an Applet on Your Page

Putting an applet on your Web page is fairly easy. You simply use the APPLET tag. You can change the applet's appearance and behavior by adjusting its parameters. Follow these steps and you will be successful in using the "BarChart" applet:

Part I—Initial Setup

1. Open the BarChart "example.html" file with your Web browser or the applet viewer.

   The path to this file is "..demo/BarChart/example.html". Make sure it works.

2. Copy the entire directory named BarChart, and place it where you can work on it.

   In this case the only file you need is Chart.class. Some applets may require many class files and may reference images, sounds, and other class files in subdirectories. As you become more familiar with Java you won't have to be this careful. But, for now, isolate the file in an empty directory

3. Open this new copy of example.html and make sure it still works. Figure 14.1 shows the bar chart.

FIG. 14.1
This is what all the fuss is about—just a bar chart. This example was chosen simply because it has a number of parameters that can be modified. You can use any applet that you like.

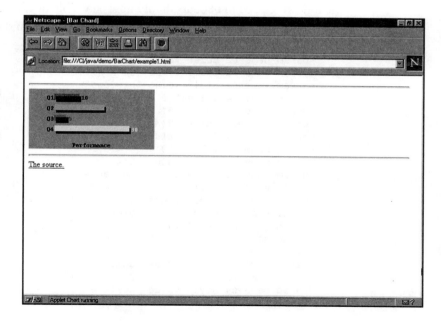

4. Place the HTML file where you want to use the Applet, and place it in the BarChart directory.

   If you don't have an HTML file, you can just open example.html and skip to Part II, step 6 below.

Part II—Copying and Pasting the Applet

1. Open "example.html" in a text editor like Notepad or SimpleText.

   This can be any word processor. Just make sure that when saving these files there is an option to save them as "text only."

2. Highlight the section of code starting with the line:

   ```
   <applet code="Chart.class" width=251 height=125>
   ```

   and ending with the line:

   ```
   </applet>
   ```

3. Copy the applet.

4. Open the HTML file that you want to insert this applet into with your text editor.

5. Set an insertion point at the place where you want to insert the applet and paste the applet.

   The following section of code should now be visible in your HTML. Make sure that you paste it somewhere between the <BODY> and </BODY> tags.

   ```
   <applet code="Chart.class" width=251 height=125>
   <param name=c2_color value="green">
   <param name=c2_label value="Q2">
   <param name=c1_style value="striped">
   <param name=c4 value="30">
   <param name=c3 value="5">
   <param name=c2 value="20">
   <param name=c4_color value="yellow">
   <param name=c1 value="10">
   <param name=c4_label value="Q4">
   <param name=title value="Performance">
   <param name=c3_style value="striped">
   <param name=columns value="4">
   <param name=c1_color value="blue">
   <param name=c1_label value="Q1">
   <param name=c3_color value="magenta">
   <param name=c3_label value="Q3">
   <param name=c2_style value="solid">
   <param name=orientation value="horizontal">
   <param name=c4_style value="solid">
   ```

```
<param name=scale value="5">
</applet>
```

6. Save your HTML as a text-only file.

Part III—Making Sure It Still Works

1. Open this new HTML file and view the applet.

N O T E If you are having problems here, it is probably because your HTML file is in the wrong directory. You can either move it to the directory where the Chart.class file is located or set a path to the Chart.class directory as specified in the next step. ■

Now that the applet works in your new HTML file you can place the applet and your HTML file anywhere you like. That is, they no longer have to be in the same directory, if you set the path to Chart.class correctly.

2. Edit the line

```
<applet code="Chart.class" width=251 height=125>
```

to reflect the new location of the class file in respect to your HTML document.

For example, if your HTML file is in a directory named "html", and if all applets are in a subdirectory named "applets", and in the applets directory you have a "BarChart" directory that holds the file "Chart.class", this first line would look like:

```
<applet code="applets/BarChart/Chart.class" width=251
height=125>
```

Anytime you change a file's relationship to another you should check it to verify the applet still works.

Modifying the Applet's Parameters

When you put in place the above applet in the previous exercise, you really didn't put any executable code there at all. You simply referenced the applet that you wanted to use, and specified a series of parameters for it. It is good programming practice for the author to give you as many controls over the applet as possible. If you have someone write an applet for you, keep this in mind. Creating a flexible applet may save you from having a second, third, and fourth applet written to do almost the exact same thing.

Part
VI

Ch
14

To modify the applet's parameters just open the HTML and start changing numbers and text strings.

The values that you can modify appear within quotation marks, so in the following line:

```
<param name=c1_color value="blue">
```

the only value that you would want to change is the text string "blue."

What parameters can you change?

Most applets come with a bit of documentation. If they don't, you can open the associated ".java" file and glean a bit of information from there.

Applet Ace and Egor—Here to Help!

Modifying parameters is not difficult. It's just a little messy. Perhaps the greatest problem with this approach is that previewing the modifications that you make are not visible quickly enough. What you would really like are sliders and color pickers attached to your applets, just like in Figure 14.2.

FIG. 14.2
It's Macromedia's Applet Ace to the rescue. Saving you from the tedium of adjusting parameters.

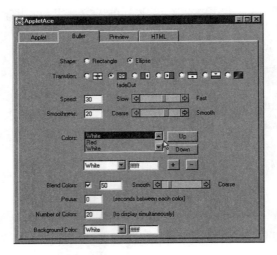

There are many products that are beginning to solve the problem of giving you interactive controls over applets. And, of course, many of these products are directed right at you, the Web developer. While these applets are certainly a trend for the future, they are currently pretty limited in the number of applets they control. Figure 14.3 is another example of an application designed to automate the process of modifying applets.

FIG. 14.3
Egor is Sausage Software's entry into the market. It lets you add images and sounds very easily.

Programmers Can Brew Their Own for Free

In a very bold and effective move to make Java a standard, Sun (the developers of Java) has been distributing the Java Developers Kit at no charge. The kit is available from their download site, and is made available to you on the CD which accompanies this book.

If you are a programmer, that is all you need to start creating applets of your own. You can modify the supplied applet, recompile them and see what you get. Once you're hooked, there are many products available that let you work in a more user-friendly environment, like the one provided by Symantec's Visual Cafe in Figure 14.4.

Part
VI

Ch
14

FIG. 14.4
Symantec's Visual Cafe provides a nice environment for the programmer, similar to products like "visual C++." These products are reasonably priced and are a very good investment, if you are going to do any Java programming.

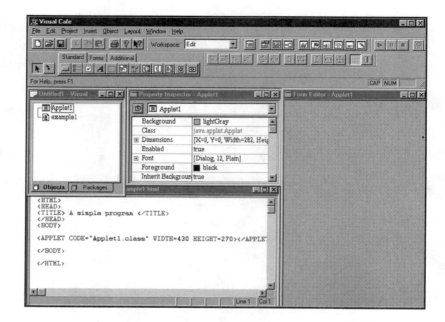

Add Zip with JavaScript

JavaScript is a scripting language that lets you add interesting, fun, and easy-to-modify snippets of code to your HTML documents. JavaScript is a scripting language in the same sense that Perl is. JavaScript is not compiled; it is always visible in human-readable form. What this means for you when you use it is that you simply place it right into your HTML document wherever you need it. There are no external files to keep track of like Java, and when what you're doing is not computationally expensive, JavaScript is a good choice. JavaScript is really ideal for helping Web designers create better, interactive Web documents.

You can see an example of JavaScript in use by looking at Chapter 9, "Attract Attention with Dynamic Pages," where JavaScript is used to animate text. Or you can look at the next section regarding cookies for a more involved example.

Using a Trail of Cookies to Track Your Users

Persistent Client State HTTP Cookies are a way of placing bits of information in your client's browser. You can then access this information as desired. Good uses for cookies include:

- Passwords

    Store your user's ID and passwords so you can access them automatically when a user logs in. The only problem with this is the cookie is held in the hand of the browser, not in the hand of the real-end user, so anyone using the browser is given access.

- Shopping carts

    When you go to Netscape and select a number of items that you want to purchase, these items are said to be "placed in your shopping cart," and indeed, when you go to check out these items are still there. How does the server know this information. In fact, it doesn't; it's your browser that carries this information because the server has defined these items as "client-side cookies." Even if you shut down your machine and go back to the site the next day, it will remember (actually your browser remembers) what you have in the shopping cart.

- Tracking visitors

    You can use cookies to find out how many times particular visitors have been to your site. Just set a cookie and index it each time the visitor shows up.

- User-defined configurations

    Are you tired of going to an Internet search page and having the wrong search engine continually selected? Well, if the Web master cared, he could set a cookie to the last search engine that you used. When you return, the state of the cookie is read, and you are given the same search engine (of course you could intentionally annoy visitors by looking at the cookie and assigning any search engine but the one they selected).

Listing 14.1 is JavaScript that sets a cookie for the number of times a user has visited a site, and displays that information to the user. It is a modification of a script

Part
VI

Ch
14

originally writen by Ryan Peters. Place it on your page and see what you need to modify.

Listing 14.1   A JavaScript Cookie that Tracks Client Visits

```
<HTML>
<HEAD>
<BODY BGCOLOR="#EEEEEE" >
<SCRIPT LANGUAGE="JAVASCRIPT">
<!--//
//Vistor's Counter
//

var t = 0;
function getCookieVal (offset) {
  var endstr = document.cookie.indexOf (";", offset);
  if (endstr == -1)
    endstr = document.cookie.length;
  return unescape(document.cookie.substring(offset, endstr));
}

function GetCookie (name) {
  var arg = name + "=";
  var alen = arg.length;
  var clen = document.cookie.length;
  var i = 0;
  while (i < clen) {
    var j = i + alen;
    if (document.cookie.substring(i, j) == arg)
      return getCookieVal (j);
    i = document.cookie.indexOf(" ", i) + 1;
    if (i == 0) break;
  }
  return null;
}

function FixCookieDate (date) {
  var base = new Date(0);
  var skew = base.getTime(); // dawn of (Unix) time - should be 0
  if (skew > 0)  // Except on the Mac - ahead of its time
    date.setTime (date.getTime() - skew);
}

function SetCookie (name, value) {
  var argv = SetCookie.arguments;
  var argc = SetCookie.arguments.length;
  var expires = (argc > 2) ? argv[2] : null;
  var path = (argc > 3) ? argv[3] : null;
  var domain = (argc > 4) ? argv[4] : null;
```

```
    var secure = (argc > 5) ? argv[5] : false;
    if (expires!=null) FixCookieDate(expires);
  //*** Uncomment this line for automatic date correction (see above)
    document.cookie = name + "=" + escape (value) +
      ((expires == null) ? "" : ("; expires=" + expires.toGMTString())) +
      ((path == null) ? "" : ("; path=" + path)) +
      ((domain == null) ? "" : ("; domain=" + domain)) +
      ((secure == true) ? "; secure" : "");
  }

    var expdate = new Date ()
    expdate.setTime (expdate.getTime() + (30 * 24 * 60 * 60 * 1000));
    // Cookie expires in 30 days.
    t = eval(GetCookie ("visits"));
    if(t==null) t=1;
    SetCookie ("visits", t + 1, expdate)
    var count = "" + t + "";

//--->

</SCRIPT>
<CENTER>
<HR SIZE=5 WIDTH=80%>
<B><FONT FACE="Comic Sans MS">Welcome, you have now visited this
<BR>page
<SCRIPT>
<!----//
     document.write (count);
//--->
</SCRIPT>
 times in the last 30 days.</FONT></B></P>
</CENTER>
<HR SIZE=3 WIDTH=60%>
</BODY>
</HTML>
```

Just as with Java, there are a lot of very nice JavaScripts out there for you to look at and play with. JavaScript is much more approachable and putting buttons and messages on your HTML documents is possible by using JavaScript.

Send a User on an Errand While You Remind Them of Home

Part
VI

Ch
14

Many times you want to give a client some important information that exists on another site. However, you do not want the information currently existing in the browser to disappear.

A good example of this would be if you had a QuickTime file located on your page. The user gets to your page and receives an error message concerning the file format of the file that they are about to view. You can send them off to Apple to pick up QuickTime 2.5, but how do you keep the current browser window open?

Your QuickTime movie reference looks like this:

```
<EMBED SRC="mymovie.mov" HEIGHT=99 WIDTH=100 PLUGINSPAGE="http://
quicktime.apple.com">
```

As described in the last chapter, if a Netscape browser does not find the appropriate plug-in, it asks users if they want to go to the location specified in PLUGINSPAGE.

So how do you keep your page from disappearing? Just add the command TARGET="framename", and a new browser window will appear. For example:

```
<EMBED SRC="mymovie.mov" HEIGHT=99 WIDTH=100 PLUGINSPAGE="http://
quicktime.apple.com" TARGET="appleqtpage">
```

N O T E It doesn't really matter what you set TARGET equal to, as long as it is not the name of an existing window as specified by the frameset command. ▪

Where to Go from Here?

Java, JavaScript, and cookies provide a powerful set of capabilities for adding interaction and interesting content to your Web pages. Things that you might find interesting include:

- ▪ Chapter 15, "CGI Scripts—Practically Cut-and-Paste City"

  These scripts can add interaction and provide forms. You'll also find a bunch of CGI scripts on the CD-ROM, so you might want to check it out.

- ▪ **www.gamelan.com**

  Includes a bunch of Java applets and JavaScripts that you will find very interesting.

- ▪ Macromedia's Applet Ace

  Check it out for controlling prebuilt applets.

CGI Scripts— Practically Cut- and-Paste City!

CGI scripts let you accomplish a bunch of diverse tasks on the Internet. In this chapter, you won't get into the details of how to program in Perl; you won't get lessons in C++ (I could use those), rather you will get a few hints and tricks that will let you start using CGI scripts immediately. On the accompanying CD you find a bunch of scripts, thanks to Matthew M. Wright. You can find out more about these scripts than you ever care to know by visiting Matt's Script Archive at: **http://worldwidemart.com/scripts.** ■

What CGI scripts are

CGI scripts allow two-way communication between the client and the server. With CGI scripts, it is not a one-way street anymore.

Why you should use CGI scripts

CGI scripts let you add animation, page counters, clocks, and all kinds of neat and useful things to your Web pages.

What tools do you need to create and modify CGI scripts

CGI scripts are practically free to create and modify. You just need a text editor, an FTP application, a good browser, and, of course, access to a server.

Look at the scripts provided for you

You've got 17 scripts courtesy of Matt's Script Archive. You can use these the way they are, or you can modify them as much as you like. Have fun.

Why Use CGI Scripts?

CGI scripts are important because they let you do a bunch of things that browsers do not do or things that browsers cannot do. In some cases, CGI scripts have been replaced by new browser capabilities. For example, image mapping (as described in Chapter 7, "Getting the Most from Clickable Image Maps") was once only available as a server-based CGI script.

Why use CGI scripts?

- They provide functionality that your browser doesn't.

  Searches, forms, and page counters are processed best by flexible, versatile, CGI scripts.

- They provide greater functionality for older browsers.

  You can provide animations and clickable image maps for users with old-technology browsers. If this is important to you, CGI scripts can be a real life saver.

- Existing scripts can be modified quickly and easily.

  There have already been hundreds of scripts written. You will be able to find existing, free scripts for some things. These scripts are usually in a format that you can modify with a text editor. So have at them!

- You can create your own scripts for special purposes.

  You can get up to your knees in programming and create your own special script to do exactly what you need them to. A financial-exchange application is included in this chapter as an example.

What Are CGI Scripts

CGI scripts are not necessarily scripts; they are really just any executable program that follows certain guidelines for input and output and is placed in the CGI-bin directory. This means that you can write CGI scripts in C, C++, or Pascal, for that matter.

Because you generally don't do very complex things with CGI scripts, it is usually easier to write them in a scripting language like Perl, cshell, or tcl. For example, all of the scripts discussed in this chapter were created in Perl.

Listing 15.1 gives you an idea of what a Perl script looks like. Almost all comments have been removed so that it will fit this page better. Normally, scripts are richly commented so that you know exactly what changing one line of code in the script will do.

Listing 15.1 An Example of Perl

```perl
#!/usr/local/bin/perl4.063 -- -*-perl-**
# Set up the webmaster mail alias
$webmaster = "webmaster@yoursite.org";
print "Content-type: text/html\n\n";
print "\n";
if ($ENV{'REQUEST_METHOD'}eq 'GET') {
    $buffer = $ENV{'QUERY_STRING'};
} else {
    read(STDIN, $buffer, $ENV{'CONTENT_LENGTH'});
}
@pairs = split(/&/, $buffer);
foreach $pair (@pairs) {
($name, $value) = split(/=/, $pair);
$value =~ tr/+/ /;
$name =~ tr/+/ /;
$value =~ s/%([a-fA-F0-9][a-fA-F0-9])/pack("C", hex($1))/eg;
$FORM{$name} = $value;
}
$YtoD = 3.00;
$PtoD = 0.05;
$MtoD = 2.50;
$FtoD = 1.60;
$DtoY = 1.0 / $YtoD;
$DtoP = 1.0 / $PtoD;
$DtoM = 1.0 / $MtoD;
$DtoF = 1.0 / $FtoD;
if ($FORM{yourCurrency}   eq "") { &req_field; exit; }
if ($FORM{amountCurrency} eq "") { &req_field; exit; }
if ($FORM{finalCurrency}  eq "") { &req_field; exit; }
if ($FORM{yourCurrency} eq "DOLLAR"){
  $commonCurrency = $FORM{amountCurrency};}
if ($FORM{yourCurrency} eq "YEN") {
  $commonCurrency = $YtoD * $FORM{amountCurrency};}
if ($FORM{yourCurrency} eq "PESO") {
```

continues

Listing 15.1   Continued

```
      $commonCurrency = $PtoD * $FORM{amountCurrency};}
if ($FORM{yourCurrency} eq "MARK") {
  $commonCurrency = $MtoD * $FORM{amountCurrency};}
if ($FORM{yourCurrency} eq "FRANC") {
  $commonCurrency = $FtoD * $FORM{amountCurrency};}
if ($FORM{finalCurrency} eq "DOLLAR"){
  $outCurrency = $commonCurrency;}
if ($FORM{finalCurrency} eq "YEN") {
  $outCurrency = $DtoY * $commonCurrency;}
if ($FORM{finalCurrency} eq "PESO") {
  $outCurrency = $DtoP * $commonCurrency;}
if ($FORM{finalCurrency} eq "MARK") {
  $outCurrency = $DtoM * $commonCurrency;}
if ($FORM{finalCurrency} eq "FRANC") {
  $outCurrency = $DtoF * $commonCurrency;}
&print_result;
exit;
sub req_field {
    print "<HTML>\n";
    print "<HEAD>\n";
    print "<TITLE>Required Field Missing</TITLE>\n";
    print "</HEAD>\n";
    print "<BODY BGCOLOR=#FFFFFF>\n";
    print "<H2>Form Error: Required Field Missing!<HR></H2>\n";
    print "<P>\n";
    print "<H3>Selections</H3><UL>\n";
    print "<LI>You Currency=$FORM{yourCurrency}\n";
    print "<LI>Currency Amount=$FORM{amountCurrency}\n";
    print "<LI>Final Currency=$FORM{finalCurrency}\n";
    print "</UL>\n";
    print "<H4>Form cannot be processed without all fields entered.</
➥H4><p>\n";
    print "\n";
    print "<P>Comments or questions regarding this website? Please send
➥mail to:</P>\n";
    print '<ADDRESS><AHREF="';
    print "MAILTO:$webmaster";
    print '"';
    print ">$webmaster </A></ADDRESS>\n";
    print "</BODY>\n";
    print "</HTML>\n";
}
sub print_result {
print "<HTML>\n";
    print "<HEAD>\n";
    print "<TITLE>Currency Exchange Results</TITLE></HEAD>\n";
    print "<BODY>\n";
    print '<a name="top"></a>';
```

```
    print "<BODY BGCOLOR=#FFFFFF>\n";
    print "<P>\n";
    print "<CENTER>\n";
    print "<H1>Currency Exchange Results</H1>\n";
    print "</CENTER>\n";
    print "<FONT SIZE=4>Following is the result of your exchange.</
➥FONT>\n";
    print "<H3>Selections</H3><UL>\n";
    print "<LI>Your Currency=$FORM{yourCurrency}\n";
    print "<LI>Currency Amount=$FORM{amountCurrency}\n";
    print "<LI>Final Currency=$FORM{finalCurrency}\n";
    print "</UL>\n";
    printf("%.2f %s equals %.2f %s.<BR>\n", $FORM{amountCurrency},
➥$FORM{yourCurrency}, $outCurrency, $FORM{finalCurrency});
    print "<BR>\n";
    print "<P>Comments or questions regarding this website? Please send
➥mail to:</P>\n";
    print '<ADDRESS><A HREF="';
    print "MAILTO:$webmaster";
    print '">';
    print "$webmaster </A></ADDRESS>";
    print "</BODY>\n";
    print "</HTML>\n";
}
```

Simple Tools for Creating and Modifying Scripts

Linking to a script is very easy. Just include a reference to the script in an HTML document. This HTML document can be a form or just a normal page; it depends on which CGI script you are using. For example, in this following HTML file:

```
<IMG SRC="store.gif"><BR>
<FONT SIZE=5>Fill out the following form to calculate an
exchange.<BR>
<FORM METHOD="POST" ACTION="../cgi-bin/exchange.pl">
<HR SIZE=5 WIDTH=350>
<CENTER>
```

You will notice the line:

```
<FORM METHOD="POST" ACTION="../cgi-bin/exchange.pl">
```

This is the line used to point to the CGI script.

> **CAUTION**
>
> The pathname to the CGI script is critical. Without it being set properly the script will not function. You should use a script that you know works, and reference it with the HTML document that you want to use. If the test script works, at least you know that the path is set correctly, your HTML document is constructed properly, and your server is processing requests properly.

Assemble the tools you need:

- Your favorite text editor, or any text editor for that matter.

  If you are using a DOS/Windows machine, the DOS Edit program is good. Qedit is a very nice DOS editor. You could use any word processor, but you have to make sure that you save your files as plain text. On the Macintosh you can use SimpleText or again, any word processor.

  And for all of those die-hard UNIX guru types, there's always vi.

- A good quick reference on the script language you are using.

  This is not necessary if you are writing a very simple script or you already are very familiar with the language you are writing in. But, it's always nice to be able to look up a command or syntax if you need to.

What Else Do You Need?

You also need access to your server's CGI-bin directory. Sometimes, your server administrator will set up a personal CGI-bin directory, where you can keep all of your personal scripts. Either way, you need access to a CGI-bin directory. Some servers don't allow users access to the CGI-bin directory, or allow only indirect access to the CGI-bin directory.

If you have no access to the CGI-bin directory, then you can forget implementing your scripts. If you have indirect access (for instance, you mail your script to a system administrator, and he or she places your script in the directory), you can still write scripts, but it's a lengthy process if you have to debug your scripts.

Your server must have access to the interpreter of the language that you choose. For instance, if you want to write in Perl, your server must have Perl.

If you choose to write your script in a compiled language, then you must make sure your program is executable on the server. If you compile it on a DOS machine, it probably won't run on a Sun-based UNIX machine.

Get Set Up For Success

Use the following method and modifying scripts is easy:

1. Find a script.

   Find an existing script that either does what you want it to do, almost does what you want it to do, or even does very little of what you want it to do (for instance, it takes input and displays output). Make sure the script is in the language that you want to work in and that it will run on your server.

2. Modify the script so that it will run on the server with minimal trouble.

   Don't sweat the details yet. Just make sure the CGI script will work on your server.

3. Next, open three windows. See Figure 15.1.

   - An FTP session to your server CGI-bin directory

   - Your editor with your script loaded

   - Your Web browser with a page that accesses the script loaded

4. Upload your script.

   On UNIX servers you'll need to make sure it has read and executed permissions, to do this, type: *chmod 755 yourscript.pl*. If you use an FTP program like WS-FTP, you may not be able to chmod your script. In this case, you'll need to telnet to the server, and chmod there (make that four windows!).

5. Test your script by using your browser.

   If the script works, you're done (unless you still have additions to make). If it doesn't, make your changes in your editor window, then upload the changes, and retest.

This works well, because you don't have to keep logging onto the server to upload your new script. Another method is to telnet to the server and use an editor like vi or emacs. But, if you like to stay away from primitive, gnarly editors, the preceding method works better.

FTP Application   Browser   Text Editor

FIG. 15.1
On a windows machine it can be Microsoft Word, CuteFTP, and Internet Explorer; on a Macintosh it can be SimpleText, Fetch, and Netscape Navigator. In any case, the secret is to have three applications open: a text editor, an FTP application, and a browser.

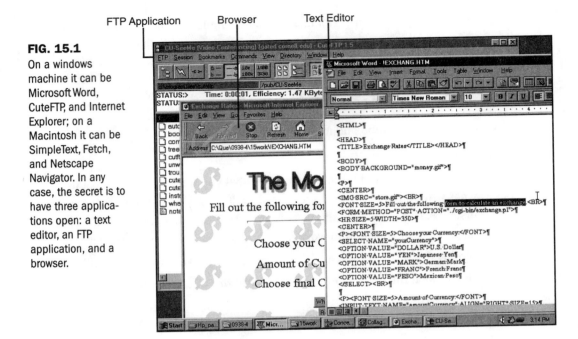

> **CAUTION**
>
> Beware of nonalphanumeric input. If you are not careful with your scripts, you can unknowingly give super-user access to your server. To prevent this, simply remove all nonalphanumeric characters from input fields before processing them.

Can Nonprogrammers Modify These?

Well, probably. With some level of computer understanding it should be fairly easy to modify field names, and to change some simple calculations. Without understanding every line in the script you should be able to change a substantial amount.

For instance, if you find a script that converts inches to centimeters, it should take little effort to modify the script to convert dollars to yen.

Make Them Look Important

Scripts can look pretty darn generic when you first find them. The fact that they are simple, out-of-the-box scripts makes them very small and easy to modify. Figure 15.2 shows an example of a generic script.

FIG. 15.2
Would anyone really bother to fill out this form?

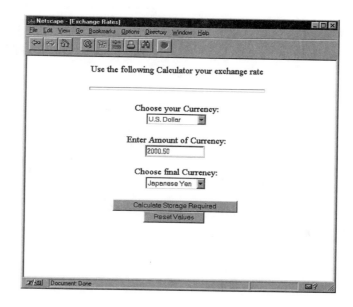

Take some time to improve the way the script looks. You should do this in two places. If the script uses a form for input, modify the HTML that contains the form so that it looks like something the user should pay attention to—like you are delivering important information. See Figure 15.3.

In the script itself the "print" commands that build the response HTML can be modified to include graphics and carefully formatted text. Let the user know that you care. In addition, place a MAILTO address and a "back" button in the output HTML. You don't want the user to sit there wondering just what the heck they should do next.

FIG. 15.3
If you provide a form that gives the user really valuable information, they will bookmark it. There is no better place to advertise for your company than on a frequently hit form.

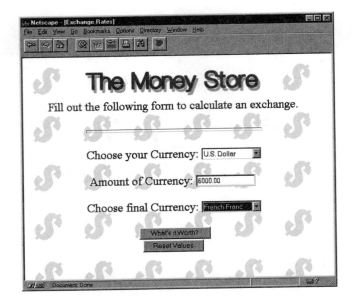

Tour de Scripts!

Here it is; what you've been waiting for—a whole bunch of script examples. There are hundreds of scripts available. Here are a few useful ones. These and others are included on the CD, so check them out.

Guestbook

This version lets users who visit your site add their name, e-mail, URL, location, and comments to a single file. New entries appear at the top of the Guestbook, giving you a historical record of those visiting your site. For an example of the Guestbook script see Figure 15.4.

Free-for-All Link Page

This *hot links* script lets users post their favorite sites to this page. You can specify categories for the links. When an URL is added it appears on the top of the page.

FIG. 15.4
Visitors can add to your Guestbook. Most people are pretty polite, just not very profound.

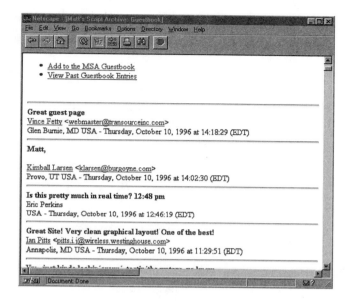

WWWBoard

WWWBoard is a threaded message board that lets users have in-depth discussions on your Web site. This script is still in an alpha state. You may want to modify it and test it thoroughly before putting it on your Web site.

Counter

This is an odometer-style, graphical counter. This counter lets you use any set of the digits available on the Net, provided they are all the same height and width. Features include transparency, color frame specifications, interlaced images, and a logging program so you can track who is visiting your site. It requires a compiled C program named "Fly" to run. See Figure 15.5 for an example of the counter script.

TextCounter

If you have Server Side Includes and are looking for a text counter, this may be for you. It can be configured to be used by an individual or a whole system; the newest version allows for file locking and padded counts. See Figure 15.5 for an example of the TextCounter script.

FIG. 15.5
This counter can display any graphical digits that you can find. I don't know what the author is saying, but he's gotten a few hits. Not much going on in Finland?

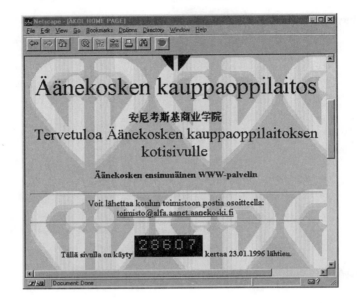

Simple Search

If you have a site with only a few hundred pages to index, the script will work for you. Simple Search allows for Boolean or switches and case sensitive or case neutral searches, and will return a list of HTML pages that match the query supplied by a user. See Figure 15.6 for an example of the Simple Search script.

FormMail

This CGI forms script will process any form, and as long as a few simple hidden configuration fields are added, the results of the form will be mailed back to you. This script lets you specify multiple recipients. It also lets you determine how you want mail sorted as it hits your mailbox.

FIG. 15.6
Most Web sites fall into the 100-300 page size range. If that is the case for your site, try Simple Search. It gives your users the type of capability they're expecting at only the best sites (like yours, right!).

HTTP Cookie Library

HTTP Cookie Library is a Perl 4 and 5 compatible library that lets you easily use Persistent Client State HTTP Cookies. You can get the cookies from the environment, prepare cookies, set cookies, change the expiration date, domain, and path all with easy subroutine calls.

Random Image Displayer

The Random Image Displayer lets you specify a list of images to be randomly displayed on your Web page, either as a background image or as an inline image on your Web page—great for employee of the week; just like in the real world though, it depends on when you look!

Server Side Includes Random Image Displayer

The Server Side Includes Random Image Displayer lets you specify alt text displayed with each image and a link that corresponds to that image. Perfect for rotating sponsors, or just for creating a surrealistic Web page.

Random Link Generator

Create a file with a bunch of your favorite URLs. Then send visitors to your Web site off in random directions.

Random Text

This requires that your server provides Server Side Includes. This is perfect for creating a quote of the day or, better yet, build a Web page on the fly with random text and images. Fun for the whole family.

TextClock

TextClock requires Side Includes. It provides readouts of times and dates in a text format. See Figure 15.7 for an example of the TextClock script.

FIG. 15.7

This shows text clock and text counter working away at the top of the page. This can be very non-obtrusive and effective.

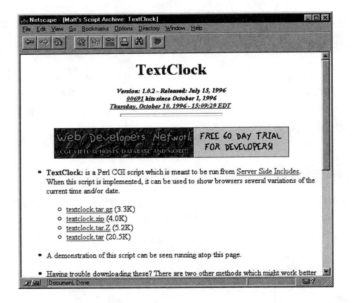

Animation

If you don't want to learn how to build animated GIFs, this could be the answer for your animation anxiety. Just plug in this script, then name a series of images so that they will be read in the proper order, and you are on your way.

Countdown

Just include the date that you want to count down to. This script will be a constant reminder that you have only two years, three months, five days, six hours, and 13 seconds until you are 40. Like sands through an hourglass, baby, there's no hope for you. Hey, it works for things like anniversaries, too! See Figure 15.8 for another example of how the Countdown script can be configured.

FIG. 15.8
It just keeps going and going, doesn't it?

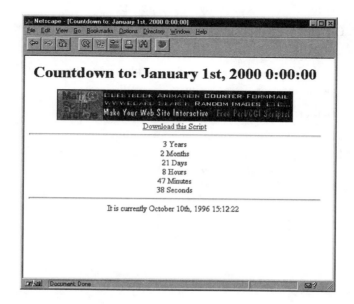

Credit Card Verifier

The Validator verifies all 13-and 16-digit Visa Cards, 16-digit MasterCards, 16-digit Novus (Discover) cards, and 15-digit American Express cards. Now, you just need a stack of cash to pay your bills.

Book 'em, Dan-O

Book 'em, Dan-O is a readily configurable, easy way to log the time of the visit, the visitor, where they came from (when used as a SSI), and what browser they were using—talk about BIG BROTHER! All great data to better refine your site! Configurable as a Server Side Include or as a "redirect," while logging the visitor.

Where to Go from Here?

The only way this stuff makes any sense is if you sit down and implement a couple of examples. Please see:

- Examples on the CD-ROM

  Look at, play with, and modify the script examples on the accompanying CD-ROM. That's the only way to get started.

- Chapter 8, "GIF Animations Are Fun and Easy"

  Server-push CGI scripts should be avoided unless you are looking for something like displaying a thousand random images. Otherwise, use GIF animations

- Chapter 14, "Java, Cookies, and Other Tricks"

  This chapter has some good information about how you can use Java, JavaScripts, and Cookies to achieve effects that duplicate or surpass the capabilities provided by CGI scripts.

A Virtual Field Trip

## CHAPTER 16

Web Master's Bag of Tricks

This is where you find a description of the tools used to build great Web pages. All you really need is a text editor and a browser (that's all some of us ever use). There are easier ways to build Web pages, and if you don't do it for a living, memorizing all those tags and thumbing through all the references can get to be a little old. So, here are some of the best shortcuts available today. Wherever possible the application programs are included on the CD-ROM that accompanies this book. ■

HTML editors

HTML editors provide ways to enter all of those HMTL tags in a more automated way.

Text converters and other utilities

You can create HTML the old-fashioned way, or you can use conversion untilities to change text from your word-processing application into HTML files.

Java and CGI script for plug and play

To delight your fans just quickly and easily modify CGI scripts and Java applets.

GIF animations

Can anything in this world really be that much fun and easy to use?

VRML—it's a far-out scene

Virtual Reality is here to stay. But, if it's not real, how do you know that it's here at all?

A slew of plug-ins

Plug-ins help expand browser capabilities. So, here's a bunch.

The Internet—The Biggest Trick of All

One of the impressive things about the Internet is the amount of powerful software that is readily available as freeware or shareware. When you have a significant task to perform while creating and editing your Web pages, remember you are not the first person to run into that problem. Look for help; you'll probably find it.

Make Document Creation and Conversion Easy

HTML itself can be one of the biggest hurdles for the creation of Web pages. There are many different applications that you can use to increase your productivity in these areas; these applications fall into about three general categories:

- HTML editors

  These editors assume you know what you're doing with HTML. Although editing and inserting tags is automated, you still should have some experience with these tags to use them properly.

- HTML translators

  These translators are great for converting word-processor files to HTML. The advantage is you can still work with your trusty word processor while writing, then fire up the translator and convert your files into HTML.

- HTML publishing applications

  Some people may call this HTML for dummies. Each application takes its own approach to hiding the intricacies of HTML from the user. At their best, these applications make Web creation easy. At their worst, these applications hide the beauty and versatility of HTML from the end user.

HTML Editors

There are probably 25 to 50 different HTML editors available today. These applications run the gamut, from programs that provide spell checking, graphic insertion, Web-site management, automatic linking, and other features to applications that will only do the simplest things like show tags in a different color. Selecting an HTML editor is a very personal choice. How do you like to work with HTML? Are you always looking to add the newest tags (even if your editor doesn't provide them); or are you happy using HTML 2.0 for the most part.

Chances are, if you bought this book, you are looking for something that will make your HTML-editing life easier while still letting you insert the newest HTML tags.

HotDog Eats 'em Up   HotDog is an extremely easy and powerful HTML editor and can be seen in Figure 16.1. It has, what amounts to, an almost completely customizable user interface. It provides a good HTML editing window; a reasonable previewing window; floating palettes with HTML tags plastered all over them; the ability to fire up the browser of your choice with the document that you're currently working on; the ability to group files into projects; table insertion; an upload button for putting your work on your server; a spelling checker that ignores tags; and an HTML verification tool that reminds you that you've forgotten the HEAD tag or misnamed it "HEADER" again!

HotDog is smart and seems to understand what you want to do. Say you have text that you have defined with the <H1> tag. In most editors, if you select the text including the tag and click the <H1>button, you end up with another pair of <H1> tags added. With HotDog the tag is toggled so that clicking the button removes the <H1> tag; click it again the <H1> tag is added. This works with all tags. What an intuitive way to assign and remove tags like bold and italic.

The first time you start up this program it comes to life with a very graphic, humorous interface; a dog is panting, and his owner is giving him orders to fetch and sit. Don't be alarmed by the "tool bone;" you can change it quickly and easily to the standard windows tool bar.

HTML Assistant   Again this is a fine HTML editor with Toolbar support for HTML 2 and HTML 3 features, including forms and tables. It has a spelling checker and an automatic HTML page creator for quick creation of new pages. It also provides the ability to extract URLs from bookmark files quickly and easily. It also has a search engine that lets you search for all the *.txt or *.htm files on your system.

FIG. 16.1

HotDog comes out of the cage in a rather bizarre configuration. However, it is extremely customizable. Even if you're one of those not so wild and crazy stock brokers, you can still configure this application so that it's not a liability to your reputation around the office.

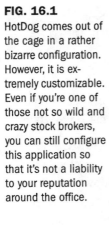
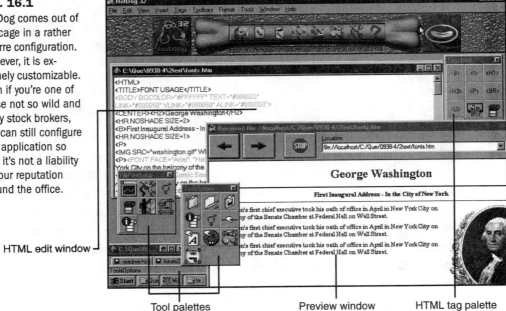

HTML edit window

Tool palettes　　　　Preview window　　　HTML tag palette

HoTMetaL HotMetal is one of the oldest and most respected HTML editors. It can be seen in Figure 16.2. It has a "semi-WYSIWYG" mode that lets you get a good idea of what the document looks like without firing up a Web browser. It has many of the features mentioned for the other two packages listed earlier in this chapter. It also recognizes and can translate the most common word processor text files. A unique feature of HoTMetal is the way it displays tags after they have been interpreted. They look like little plastic labels instead of like-editable text. Of course, you can enter a mode where the tags are editable as well. Its frames editor is very nice, and it provides a ton of templates, letting you create HTML documents that look good in a hurry.

One of the true advantages of HoTMetal is it runs on Windows 95, Windows 3.X, Macintosh, and UNIX workstations. So, if you have to move from workstation to workstation, you can always find a familiar face if you know how to use HoTMetaL.

FIG. 16.2
HoTMetaL provides a no-nonsense, easy-to-use interface. The way it displays tags is unique. Its ability to run on multiple platforms is laudable.

Tags look like tags ——

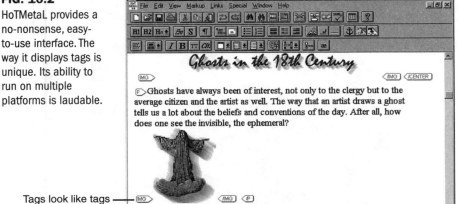

Part
VII

Ch
16

HTML Translators

HTML translators are the little extensions that you can get to either "plug in" to your word processor or are designed to provide stand-alone conversion. Here the trick is to find the right converter. Many powerful word processors have these features built in. Two that come to mind are FrameMaker's HTML converter and Microsoft's Internet Assistant, which can be seen in Figure 16.3. Internet Assistant is actually available in several flavors, so you can get it for Microsoft Word and Excel. These are very convenient utilities, particularly if you have a lot of legacy documents that you need to get online. If these documents are created with style sheets, the translators can actually do a very nice job. However, if style sheets are not used, this isn't much better than saving them as plain-text files and opening them up with an HTML editor.

HTML for Complete Idiots, or Is This the Future?

It was not long ago that when people talked about HTML editors, they were actually talking about little applications like Notepad or SimpleText. Well, things have changed, as can be seen by looking at Microsoft FrontPage in Figure 16.4. There are a number of commercial applications that are struggling to be king of the hill in the battle to become the standard HTML publishing application. The big boys like Claris, Microsoft, and Adobe all have applications on the market that challenge the feature set of desktop publishing applications.

FIG. 16.3
It's a Word Processor. It's a Web browser. It's an HTML editor.

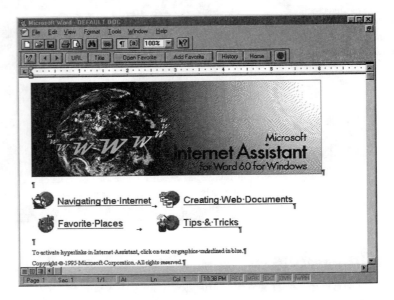

FIG. 16.4
Microsoft's FrontPage provides an HTML editor, a local server, and a Web management module. It's a great way to get started.

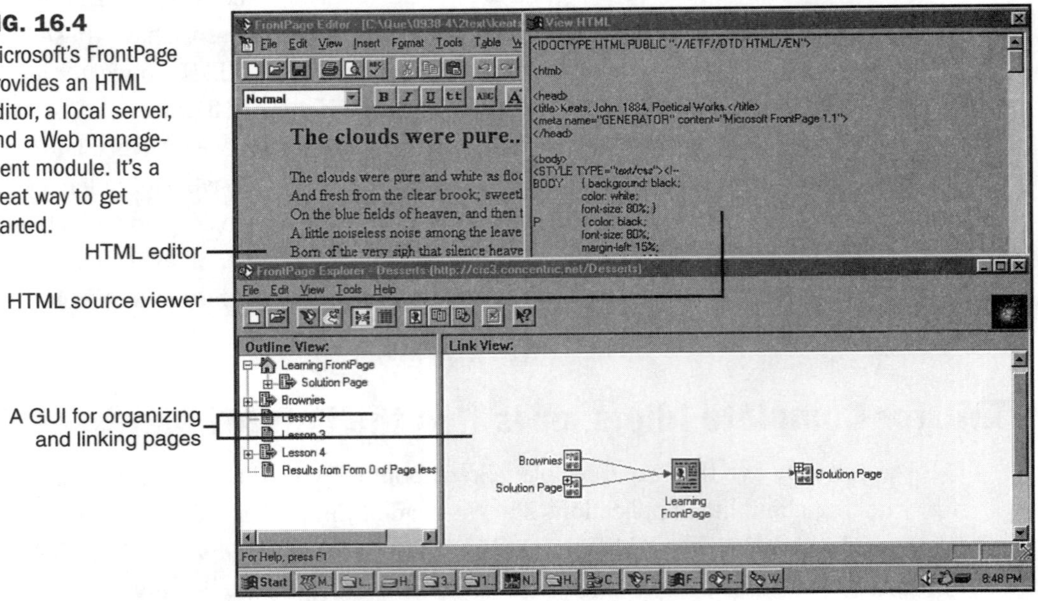

HTML editor ——

HTML source viewer ——

A GUI for organizing and linking pages ——

So what's the problem with these applications if they're so easy to use and so powerful? Yes, you can really whip HTML documents together quickly with these applications. Most people have one of the following views:

- People shouldn't care about HTML as long as their pages look OK.

  These people view HTML as kind of a PostScript. That is, even if you don't know anything about PostScript files (when was the last time you whipped out your text editor and started hacking on a PostScript file?) you still can create wonderful, full-featured PostScript documents.

- People should know how to use HTML.

  This group has been around HTML long enough to know that it seems like new tags are added every couple of weeks. Purchasing one of these products still doesn't solve all of your problems or let you do everything you want.

- I'm not going to spend a hundred bucks on an HTML editor.

  Well, these folks probably aren't really good about paying for all of their shareware applications either. These people can be won over if these applications deliver on their promises of increased productivity and more compliant HTML code.

Where do you fit in? Take a look at these applications. Most of them take a stab at solving a host of Web-site related problems. And many are almost shareware in nature. That is, you can get a free 30 day trial.

N O T E Use of these new HTML publisher applications has a couple of problems. Any attempt at a WYSIWYG display will be imperfect while Netscape and Microsoft keep adding extensions. This problem can be reduced by using the Internet for frequent software downloads, but that will not completely eliminate this problem.

There is a troubling trend that can be seen in some of these applications; that is their attempt to completely eliminate any references to HTML. For example, one application has buttons at the top of the page that apparently change the font size. The buttons read Larger / Smaller. So you would assume that they are changing the <FONT SIZE=X> tag. But, when you look to see what is being affected, you notice that this button actually changes font size by using the <H1>, <H2>, and <H3> tags. These particular tags have great historical importance and are interpreted by some of the older browsers in very specific ways. These differences are sure to be worked out in the future, but this surely shows the awkward stage that these applications are going through. ■

What Does the Future Hold?

These applications will grow in popularity; a few of the most popular shareware applications will become bigger and more commercial. All word processors and desktop publishing applications will support HTML and HTML conversion much more efficiently. HTML itself will change and begin to stabilize. HTML is still just a baby.

Pump Up with CGI Scripts and Java Applets

CGI scripts let you put page counters, guest books, animations, and lots of other cool things on your Web pages. We have included almost 20 CGI scripts from one of the most popular sites on the Web, Matt's Script Archive at **http://worldwidemart.com/scripts/**. There is more information about these scripts and how to use them in Chapter 15, "CGI Scripts—Practically Cut-and-Paste City."

Java is the hottest topic on the Net. If you really want to impress your friends and loved ones, just plop a couple of these babies on your Web page and watch your page counter burn a hole in your screen! Java applets are easier to configure and even cooler than CGI scripts. We've provided a bunch of applets for you on the CD. Also check out **http://www.gamelan.com**. Here folks from all over the world meet, talk about, and distribute Java code. There's nothing like carefully brewed Java to make good friends.

GIF Animations—An 11 on a 10-Point Scale

This is the one thing that you need to know how to do. And it is strange that for a long time these animations received so little notice. The secret lies in the ability to store more than one image in a GIF file. The old GIF file format gets banged around with its limitation to 256 colors, but it lets you animate with the greatest of ease. Check out Chapter 8, "GIF Animations Are Fun and Easy," for everything that you ever wanted to know about GIF animations. All you need is GIFBuilder if you're on the Macintosh or the GIF Construction Kit if you're running windows. Both work great, and they're on the CD.

2D Today, 3-Space Tomorrow

3D modeling has been around for a long time; early on for CADCAM and scientific research, then for photo-realistic rendering and 3D animation (actually the 3D-animation part happened first, you just didn't see any of it for a long time). Now, you can see it spread all over the Internet. VRML is really a topic too specialized and too detailed to be covered adequately in this book. There are some pretty sophisticated VRML worlds available for your viewing on the Internet, as can be seen in Figure 16.5. However, you can download some models, stick them on your pages, and even modify these models and their textures with the tools that we are providing here.

On the CD you will find Paragraph's Virtual Home Space Builder. It is really a very nice, professional application that will let you get your feet wet with this technology over the course of an afternoon. Most advanced 3D modeling software requires weeks, if not months, of training before you start to catch on. Try it.

FIG. 16.5
It's still hard to believe that you can put something this nice on your Web page and let people interact with it. Now, any of us can afford a trip to see Die Walkure.

Get Plugged In with Plug-Ins

As you're wandering around the Web, there is nothing more frustrating than getting to content that you cannot see because you don't have the latest plug-ins. So, we've provided you with a healthy bunch of plug-ins to get started with.

Where to Get the Hottest Goods

The reason you go to school is to learn how to learn. The reason you use a Web browser is to download more software that you can use with your Web browser. Here are some places that you can go to download a bunch of cool software:

http://www.tucows.com

http://www.shareware.com

To get your hands on public domain literature and images, you should check out Savetz's Unofficial Internet Public Domain Index at:

HTTP//www.northcoast.com/savetz/pd/pd.html

As the title indicates, this is not so much a source for Public Domain content as it is a reference to Web sites that have lots and lots of cool pictures and literature. Everything from Shakespeare to Jupiter fly-bys can be found by looking at this wonderful index.

Acrobat Lets You Juggle Huge Documents with the Greatest of Ease

Have you ever tried to put an entire user's manual online, complete with color pictures, and tried to deliver it to your customers in a format that they could easily browse and print out? HTML is very good at what it does, but it isn't very good at that.

Adobe, the developers of PostScript many moons ago, has a series of products that can be used to convert sophisticated documents from PostScript into a format called the Portable Document Format (PDF). The nice thing about this format is that since it is PS it guarantees exactly what each page will look like (just like it does in your word-processing application).

These files can then be put on the Internet and viewed by folks who have Adobe Acrobat Reader (a freely distributed product that can be seen in Figure 16.6). If you are using a desktop publishing application like FrameMaker, it will actually save a bunch of Acrobat information that can be used in the PDF file. Your headings will be converted to hypertext links that reference the appropriate content. If you have documents that you need to publish as hard copy, be distributed on disk as help files, and placed on the Internet for browsing, take a look at Adobe at:

http://www.adobe.com

You are provided with Adobe Acrobat Reader, which lets you view PDF documents on your local system or on the Internet.

FIG. 16.6
Acrobat Reader fits right into your browser. This technology has gotten so much better over the last year that you won't recognize it if you haven't seen it in a while.

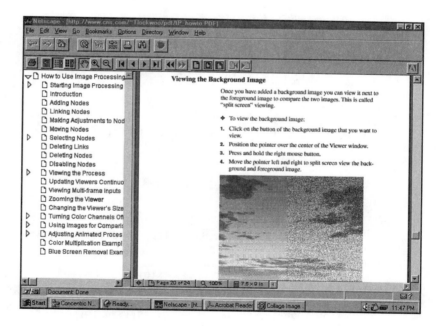

Fading a BackGround In and Out

And finally, here is a JavaScript (Listing 16.1) that can be modified as you like to create a background that fades from one color to another. You can adjust both the colors and the speed of the fades by modifying this script. Hints for modifying this script are included; just see the comments beginning with the phrase /* Usage. You can copy this script from the CD-ROM and include it in your pages.

Listing 16.1—The Fade in, Fade out, JavaScript.

```
<SCRIPT LANGUAGE="JavaScript">

/*  Fade Script v0.1 by Kouichirou@Eto.com 1996

 * Copyright (c) 1996 Kouichirou Eto. All Rights Reserved.
 * You can freely copy, use, modify this script,
 * if the credit is given in the source.
 * If you would like to get information for this script,
 * please access <http://eto.com/JavaScript/>

 */
function makearray(n) {
    this.length = n;
    for(var i = 1; i <= n; i++)
        this[i] = 0;
    return this;
}
hexa = new makearray(16);
for(var i = 0; i < 10; i++)
    hexa[i] = i;
hexa[10]="a"; hexa[11]="b"; hexa[12]="c";
hexa[13]="d"; hexa[14]="e"; hexa[15]="f";
function hex(i) {
    if (i < 0)
        return "00";

    else if (255 < i)
        return "ff";
    else
        return "" + hexa[Math.floor(i/16)] + hexa[i%16];
}
function setbgColor(r, g, b) {
    var hr = hex(r); var hg = hex(g); var hb = hex(b);
    document.bgColor = "#"+hr+hg+hb;
}
function fade(sr, sg, sb, er, eg, eb, step) {
    for(var i = 0; i <= step; i++) {
        setbgColor(
        Math.floor(sr * ((step-i)/step) + er * (i/step)),
        Math.floor(sg * ((step-i)/step) + eg * (i/step)),
        Math.floor(sb * ((step-i)/step) + eb * (i/step)));
    }
}
```

```
/* Usage:
 *   fade(inr,ing,inb, outr,outg,outb, step);
 * example.
 *   fade(0,0,0, 255,255,255, 255);
 * fade from black to white with very slow speed.
 *   fade(255,0,0, 0,0,255, 50);
 *   fade(0xff,0x00,0x00, 0x00,0x00,0xff, 50); // same as above
 * fade from red to blue with fast speed.
 * step 2 is very fast and step 255 is very slow.
 */
function fadein() {
    fade(255,255,255, 0,0,0, 120);
}
function fadeout() {
    /*fade(0,0,0, 255,255,255, 120); */
}
/* do fadein */
fadein();
/***** end fade script *****/



</SCRIPT>
```

Where to Go from Here?

Now Web master, you should be fully armed to head out into the world and create some truly impressive Web pages. However, you might want to take a look through the upcoming Web Gallery to see some of the brightest sights of the Internet.

## CHAPTER 17

Web Gallery

There are many sites on the Web with important content, but only so many official whiz bang sites. Take some time to check out these sites; you're sure to find useful information, pick up some tricks and tips, and just have fun. You'll see why the sites in this chapter were chosen.

This is cutting edge VRML, including dependencies, behaviors, and so on. ■

See whiz bang Web sites

The sites in this chapter contain elements that you have covered in this book. There is nothing more educational than going to a cool site and clicking the View Source button. You've no doubt found some of your favorite tricks that way.

Check out cool content

Many of the sites in this chapter have very recent types of content, so that you can test the state of your plug-ins by visiting them.

You can look to the future

Most of the sites in this chapter contain types of data and types of user interfaces that are beyond the normal Web page of today. Looking at these sites will wake you up!

Have some fun!

We've all done it, been on the phone with someone and said "Hey, have you checked out the stuff on www.coolsite.com?" Well, if it was true yesterday, it's more true today. The sites in this chapter just keep getting cooler and cooler.

www.vtourist.com

It's a clickable image map of the world. Go to your favorite places. See your favorite sites. It's all part of the Virtual Tourist II site (see Figure 17.1).

FIG. 17.1
This clickable image map of the world tells you all you need to know. Click here to go there.

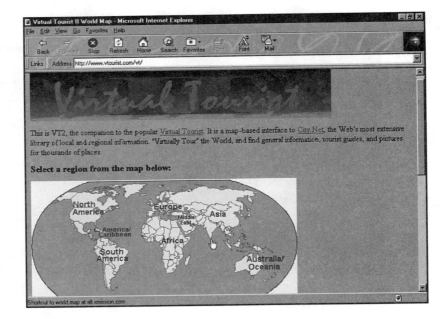

www.sportsline.com

You can go here to get your sports fix. The site is laid out nicely by using tables. It's a graphically rich page that doesn't take all that long to download. Another cool feature is the Live Radio section, where you can listen to sporting events live (see Figure 17.2).

vrml.sgi.com

Silicon Graphics manufactures powerful, UNIX graphics workstations. But, more importantly, SGI provides tools for artists, scientists, and engineers to produce 3D content. So, it's not surprising to see some terrific 3D VRML content at this Web site. Note: SGI has a VRML plug-in for Netscape that is already VRML 2.0 compliant. Not only are the VRML worlds nice, but the use of frames is very effective (see Figure 17.3).

FIG. 17.2
Good use of tables, buttons, and RealAudio radio feeds makes this site well worth a visit.

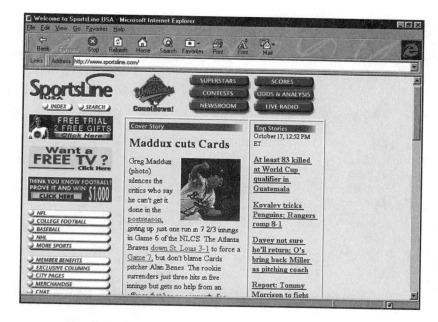

FIG. 17.3
Not only is this site designed well, it also contains lots of good information and content based on the very latest VRML technologies.

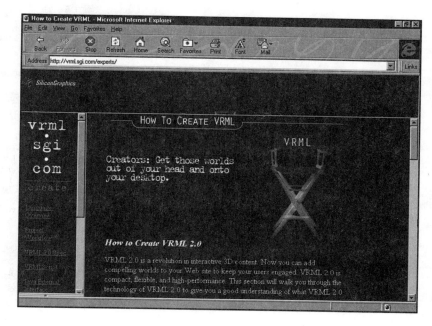

www.planet9.com

Planet nine is really more like planet three, Earth! This place has some of the most detailed and interesting VRML scenes that you will find anywhere. Many cities are modeled. In addition, a Virtual Soma exists so that you can explore the streets and shops of this San Francisco neighborhood (see Figure 17.4).

FIG. 17.4
Visit Virtual Soma to check out an art show or grab a cup of coffee at their virtual cafe.

www.paragraph.com

ParaGraph is a leading developer of VRML technologies like Virtual Home Space Builder. Their graphic design is nice. They also have a "virtual home page," so that you can visit their site in 3D mode (see Figure 17.5).

www.espn.com

ESPN is the largest sports broadcasting network in the country. Their Web site lives up to this heritage. ESPN generally has Java applets that update scores or other cool things that you can actually place on your desktop. These little scoreboards don't disappear when you leave their page. Another thing that you should check out is the mixture of free information with content that they charge for. They have QuickTime movies and RealAudio content available, but they usually charge for it. In addition, they have special sections for handicapping events or other insider features that you have to be a member to see. However, there is still lots of good information available for the sports bum without a Web coin to his name (see Figure 17.6).

FIG. 17.5
On this page there are a lot of models that you can download. Notice how they are effectively grouped in this table.

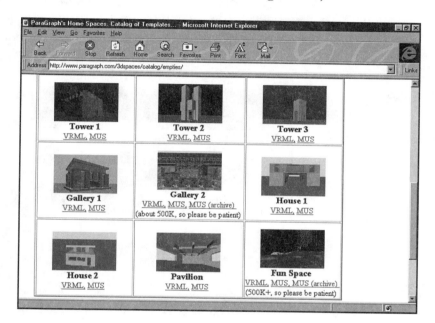

FIG. 17.6
Effective layout, applets, and a ton of data handled elegantly makes this site a model in many respects.

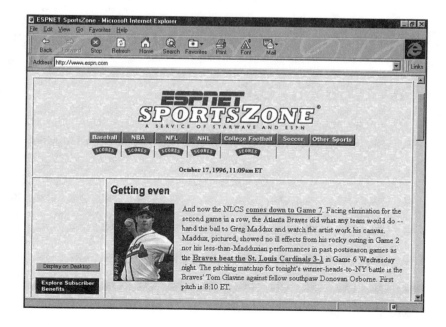

www.detnews.com

The Detroit News is a very nice example of an online newspaper. The front page and each section header is carefully laid out by using tables. However, when you get to individual articles they are just plain text with an occasional picture. This is a good compromise between an attractive and graphical rich newspaper, and one that downloads quickly but is not formatted for easy access and quick downloads (see Figure 17.7).

FIG. 17.7
The Detroit News online—weather, sports, even the debate.

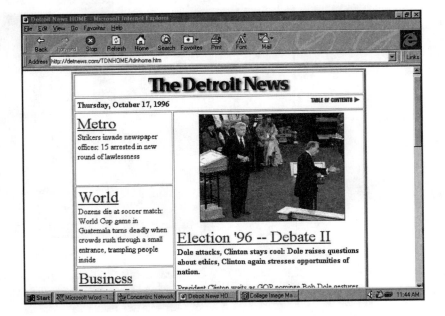

www.fedex.com

Federal Express's original home page was graphically barren, but it got right down to asking you what you wanted. The new site suffers from graphic overload. The front page is beautiful, kind of a FEDEX in space motif, but it takes too long to download. Fortunately, they put plain-text buttons along the bottom of the page that let you jump to the section where you need to go. Fill out the online form, and you don't have to fill out a paper air bill. Fill out the online form, and you don't have to call their 800 number. Very nice (see Figure 17.8).

FIG. 17.8
Fill out this form, and
you are ready for a
pick up!

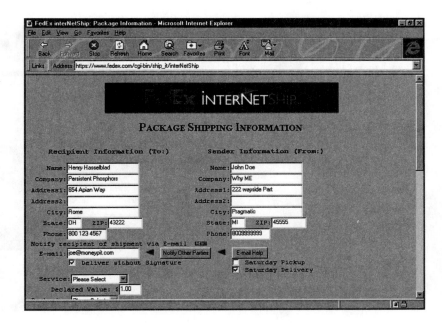

the-tech.mit.edu/KTP/Gallery/
gallery.html

This is a gallery of cool, computer-generated art. Kai's power tools are a product
that lets you perform all kinds of deformations and effects on images. Their pages
take advantage of many tricks in this book. In addition, they have a very nice educational section regarding how to create images and other content for the Web
(see Figure 17.9).

FIG. 17.9
A table of cool pictures. Keep working, and you'll be in their hall of fame someday.

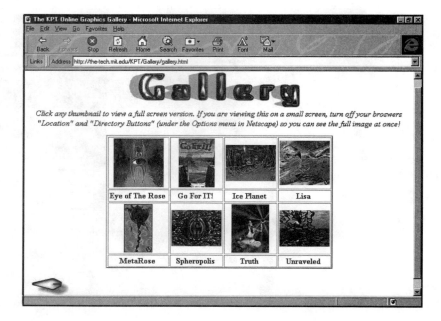

edcwww.cr.usgs.gov

Well, whatever that URL is, this is the home of the Global Land Information System provided by the United States Geological Survey. Of course, the satellite photos are nice, but the layout for this page is very effective. It is not really fancy, but it does convey a lot of information in a very effective manner. Keep this type of setup in mind for doing work for customers that want something nice but are either limited to very few graphics by bandwidth issues or simply cannot afford a bunch of graphics work (see Figure 17.10).

www.internet.com

Looking for some RAM? Need a printer? This site has a bunch of stuff. Check out the multiple-column layout, the search capability and the ability to buy stuff online (see Figure 17.11).

FIG. 17.10
There is a lot of information on these pages. In some cases the greatest challenges facing a Web designer is the organization of vast amounts of information.

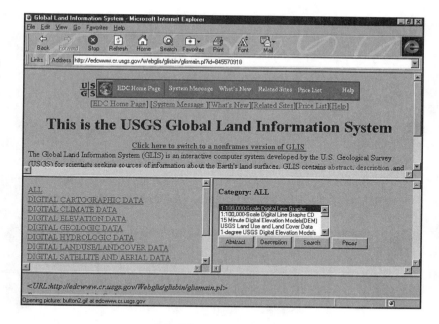

FIG. 17.11
Is there any way to set a book mark that my browser is not allowed to visit? You could spend way too much money here.

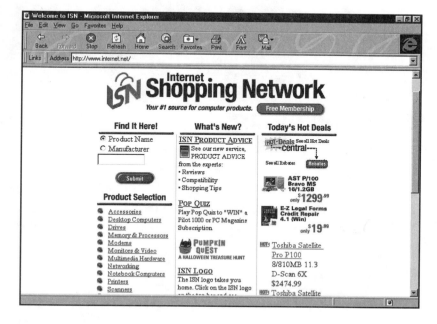

www.musicblvd.com

This place literally rocks! Nice graphics and the ability to order music online just isn't enough. The designers here have been thoughtful enough to make music available in two versions of RealAudio and MPEG (see Figure 17.12).

FIG. 17.12
Music Boulevard,
walk this way to the
music store of
tomorrow.

www.thinker.org

This is an archive of 60,000 pieces of art. Now, this is a truly worthy application of Internet technology. Not only is the archive impressive, but the overall design is a perfect blend of white space with graphic accents. Look at how little of the page is actually made up of graphics. However, the overall impact is striking—I guess that's what happens when you get artists involved with projects like this (see Figure 17.13).

www.ran.org

This place feels like a political action committee with a social conscience. You can see a Shockwave movie, QuickTime movies, and learn all kinds of interesting things about environmental issues. In addition, they provide a service that lets you send FAXs to policy makers (see Figure 17.14).

FIG. 17.13
As soon as I finish this chapter I'm going to spend some time nosing around this museum. This is truly the Web at its best.

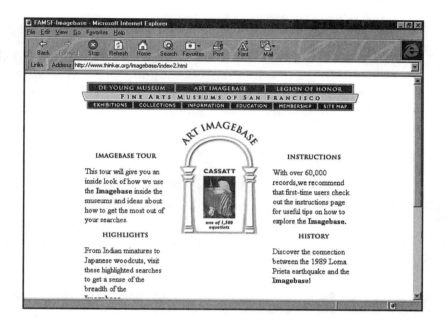

FIG. 17.14
The interesting graphics and content-rich pages keep this site from being too preachy.

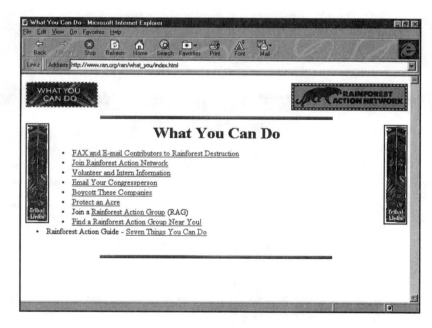

www.prognet.com

This is the RealAudio page. It looks good and sounds better. Of course, you can get the latest players, and so on, from this page. In addition, there are links to good sites across the country. Notice how graphics and linking with other locations are handled so effortlessly (see Figure 17.15).

www.mapquest.com

MapQuest (see Figure 17.16) provides one of the most useful services available. Maps, maps, and more maps. You can enter someone's address, anywhere, and get a map of their town or even their neighborhood. In addition, you can enter a "from" and "too" location and receive detailed instructions on how to get there. It provides an online trip ticket that takes only seconds to generate!

www.alias.com

Alias (see Figure 17.17) is a 3D computer graphics company that provides solutions to the highest paid and most talented 3D designers and animators in the world. As you may guess, their Web site contains striking imagery. They don't mess around when it comes to graphic design either.

FIG. 17.15
You would expect this site to show some Web savvy, and it does.

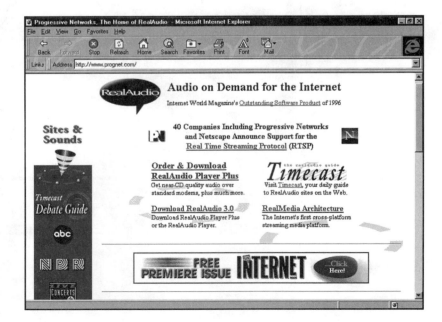

FIG. 17.16
Yes, I actually use this site when I'm going to drive from Saint Charles, Michigan to Belle Isle, Florida.

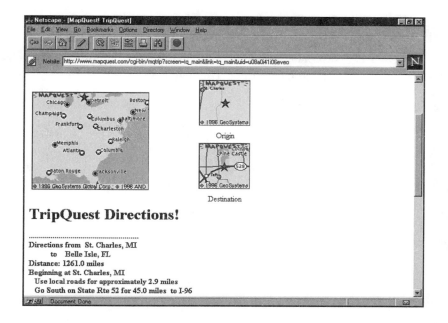

FIG. 17.17
Like some eye candy? Try **http:// www.alias.com.** Here, they will teach you how to build a photo-realistic mountain range—way, way, cool.

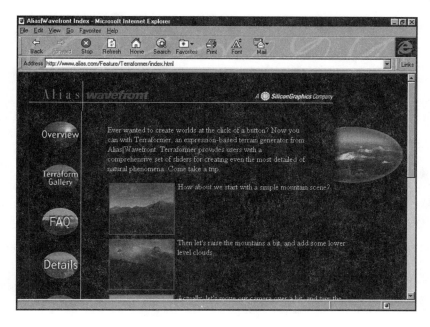

Part
VII

Ch
17

Where to Go from Here?

Well, you certainly have enough to do, enough tools to be effective, and even some hints on good places to go. Good luck on your Web adventures!

Appendixes

HTML Tags

All tags and their parameter listings are based on the HTML 3.2 standard unless otherwise indicated. Netscape specific tags and parameters are noted by [N] and MS Internet Explorer specific tags are noted by [M]. Visit the World Wide Web Consortium (W3C) home page at **www.w3.org**, for information about the HTML 3.2 standard. More information on Netscape specific tags can be found at Netscape's site: **www.netscape. com**. Microsoft Internet Explorer tags are covered at Microsoft's IE site: **www.microsoft.com/ie/**. ■

Open Tag	Parameters	Closing Tag
<!—	*comment*	—>

<a>	name = *"anchorname"*
	href = *"url"*
	        "url#anchorname"
	        "url?cgivariables"
	target = *"windowname"*
	rel = *"relationship"*
	title = *"titletext"*
		</a>

<address>		</address>

<applet>	alt = *"text"*
	align = absbottom
	        absmiddle
	        baseline
	        bottom
	        left
	        middle
	        right
	        texttop
	        top
	code = *"filename"*
	codebase = *"filepath"*
	height = *pixels*
	width = *pixels*
	hspace = *pixels*
	vspace = *pixels*
	name = *"appletname"*
		</applet>

<area>	alt = *"text"*
	coords = *"x1,y1"*,
	            "x2,y2"…
	shape = rect
	        circle
	        polygon
	href = *"url"*
	nohref
		none

<b>		</b>
<base>	href = *"url"* target = *"windowname"* [N]	none

Open Tag	Parameters	Closing Tag
<basefont>^M	color = "color" name = "fontname" size= n	
<big>		</big>
<bgsound>^M	loop = # infinite/-1 src = "url"	none
<blink>		</blink>
<blockquote>		</blockquote>

<body>	alink = "#RRGGBB"
	background = "url"
	bgcolor = "#RRGGBB"
	    aqua
	    black
	    blue
	    fuchsia
	    gray
	    green
	    lime
	    maroon
	    navy
	    olive
	    purple
	    red
	    silver
	    teal
	    white
	    yellow
	bgproperties = fixed^M
	link = "#RRGGBB"
	text = "#RRGGBB"
	vlink = "#RRGGBB"
		</body>

	clear = left
	    right
	    all
		none

<center>		</center>

continues

continued

Open Tag	Parameters	Closing Tag
<cite>		</cite>
<code>		</code>
<dd>		next line break
<dfn>		</dfn>
<dir>		</dir>
<div>	align = center left right	</div>
<dl>		</dl>
<dt>		next line break
<em>		</em>
<embed>	parameters (plug-in specific) src = *"url"* height = *pixels* width = *pixels*	none
<font>	color = *"#RRGGBB"* aqua black blue fuchsia gray green lime maroon navy olive purple red silver teal white yellow face = <fontname>M size = *fontsize* +/- *fontsize*	</font>

Open Tag	Parameters	Closing Tag

\<form\>	action = *"url"*
	method = get
	       post
	enctype = "application/x-www-form-urlencoded"
	      "multipart/form-data"
		\</form\>

\<frame\>	marginheight =
	   pixels
	marginwidth =
	   pixels
	frameborder = *"yes"*
	     = *"no"*
	border = *"pixels"*
	bordercolor = *"color"*
	name = *"windowname"*
	    "_blank"
	    "_self"
	    "_parent"
	    "_top"
	noresize
	scrolling = yes
	    no
	    auto
		src = *"url"* none

\<frameset\>[N]	cols = *"width1,*
	    width2,..."
	  "width1%,
	    width2%,..."
	rows = *"height1,*
	    height2,..."
	  "height1%,
	    height2%,..."*
		\</frameset\>

\<h1\>	align = center
	    left
	    right
		\</h1\>

\<h2\>	align = center
	    left
	    right
		\</h2\>

continues

continued

Open Tag	Parameters	Closing Tag
\<h3>	align = center left right	\</h3>
\<h4>	align = center left right	\</h4>
\<h5>	align = center left right	\</h5>
\<h6>	align = center left right	\</h6>
\<head>		\</head>
\<hr>	size = *pixels* [N] width = *pixels* [N] *window%* noshade	none
\<html>		\</html>
\<i>		\</i>
\<img>	src = *"url"* alt = *"text"* border = *"width"* controls[M] loop = *#*[M] infinite/-1 loopdelay = *seconds*[M] start = fileopen[M] mouseover lowsrc = *"url "* height = *pixels* hspace = *pixels* width = *pixels* vspace = *pixels* units = *units* align = top middle bottom	none

Open Tag	Parameters	Closing Tag
	ismap usemap = *"url#name"*	

<input>	type = *"text"*
	    "password"
	    "checkbox"
	    "radio"
	    "submit"
	    "reset"
	    "file"
	    "image"
	    "jot"
	    "scribble"
	    "range"
	    "hidden"
	name = *"inputname"*
	value = *"text"*
	checked
	size = *"width"*
	maxlength = *"length"*
	min = *rangemin*
	max = *rangemax*
	accept = *mediatypes*
		none

<isindex>		none
<kbd>		</kbd>
<li>		next line break
<link>	rev = *"relationship"* rel = *"relationship"* href = *"url"*	none
<listing>		</listing>
<map>	name = *"url "*	</map>

<marquee>*M	align = bottom
	       middle
	       top
	behavior = scroll
	         alternate
	         slide
		</marquee>

continues

continued

Open Tag	Parameters	Closing Tag

	bgcolor = *"#RRGGBB"*
	direction = right
	        left
	height = *pixels*
	       window%
	hspace = *pixels*
	loop = #
	    infinite/-1
	scrollamount = *pixels*
	scrolldelay = *milliseconds*
	vspace = *pixels*	

<menu>	align = center
	      justify
	      left
	      right
	compact
		</menu>

<meta>	content = # http-equiv = *attrib* refresh[N] name = *"metaname"* url = *"url"*	none
<multicol>[N]	cols = n gutter = *"pixels"* width = *"pixels"*	</multicol>
<nobr>		</nobr>
<noemed>[N]		</noemed>
<noframes>[N]		</noframes>

<object>[M]	align = left
	     texttop
	     middle
	     textmiddle
	     baseline
	     textbottom
	     center
	     right
		</object>

Open Tag	Parameters	Closing Tag
	border =n	
	classid = *"url"*	
	codebase = *"url"*	
	codetype = codetype	
	data = *"url"*	
	declare	
	height =n	
	hspace =n	
	name = *"url"*	
	notab	
	shapes	
	standby = *"message"*	
	tabindex =n	
	title = *"text"*	
	type = *"type"*	
	usemap = *"url"*	
	vspace =n	
	width =n	
<ol>	align = center	</ol>
	justify	
	left	
	right	
	compact	
	start = #	
	type = A^N	
	a	
	I	
	i	
	1	
<option>	disabled	</option>
	selected	
	value = *"variable"*	
<p>	align = center	none
	left	
	right	
<param>	name = *"paramname"*	none
	value = *"value"*	

continues

continued

Open Tag	Parameters	Closing Tag
<plaintext>		none
<pre>		</pre>
<s>		</s>
<samp>		</samp>
<script>	language = *scripting language* src = *filename* type = *MIME type*	</script>

<select>	align = left
	    middle
	    right
	    top
	disabled
	height = *pixels*
	    window%
	multiple
	name = "*selectname*"
	size = "#"
	src = "*url*"
	units = *units*
	width = *pixels*
	multiple
		</select>

<small>		</small>

<spacer>[N]	type = "horizontal"
	    "vertical"
	    "block"
	size = "*pixels*"
	width = "*pixels*"
	height = "*pixels*"
		none

<strike>		</strike>
<strong>		</strong>
<style>	title = *title* type = *MIME type*	</style>
_{		}

Open Tag	Parameters	Closing Tag
^{		}
<table>	align = bleedleft[NM]	</table>
	bleedright[NM]	
	center	
	left	
	right	
	justify	
	border = #	
	cellpadding = #	
	cellspacing = #	
	cols = #	
	frame = above	
	below	
	border	
	box	
	hsides	
	lhs	
	rhs	
	void	
	vsides	
	noflow	
	nowrap	
	rules = all	
	basic	
	cols	
	none	
	rows	
	units = en	
	pixels	
	relative	
	width = *pixels*	
	"percentage%"	
<td>	align = center	</td>
	left	
	right	
	valign = baseline	
	bottom	
	middle	
	top	

continues

continued

Open Tag	Parameters	Closing Tag
	bgcolor = "#rrbbgg"[M] colspan = # rowspan = # width = *pixels*[N]	
\<textarea>	name = *"textname"* rows = "#" cols = "#"	\</textarea>

\<th>	align = center
	  left
	  right
	valign = baseline
	  bottom
	  middle
	  top
	bgcolor = "#rrbbgg"[M]
	colspan = #
	rowspan = #
	width = *pixels*[N]
		\</th>

\<title>		\</title>

\<tr>	align = center
	  left
	  right
	valign = baseline
	  bottom
	  middle
	  top
		\</tr>, next
		\</tr>, or
		\</table>

\<tt>		\</tt>
\<u>		\</u>
\<ul>		\</ul>
\<var>		\</var>
\<wbr>		none
\<xmp>		\</xmp>

Glossary of Terms

Aifc (also referred to as Aiff-c)   A compressed version of Aiff.

AIFF   A format common on Silicon Graphics UNIX workstations and Apple Macintosh computer systems. It allows a variety of recording rates and bits. This format is supported by most browsers.

Applet   A small application written in the Java programming language that requires a browser or other special applications to run properly.

ASCII (American Standard Code for Information Interchange)   The world-wide standard for code numbers used by computers to represent all the upper and lowercase Latin letters, numbers, punctuation, and so on.

Au   An audio format that provides a 2:1 compression ratio and is similar in quality and file size to the Aiff and Wav formats. Au is a format originally employed on NEXT and Sun workstations. It is a very popular format and is supported by most browsers.

Backbone   A high-speed line that forms a major route for information within a network.

Bandwidth   A measure of how much information can be sent through any given connection. Bandwidth is usually measured in bits per second.

Baud   Commonly used as a measure for how many bits a modem can send or receive per second.

Binhex (from BINary HEXadecimal)   A method of converting nontext files (nonASCII) into ASCII.

Border   An attribute of the IMG tag that specifies the width of the border that surrounds a particular image. In the command <IMG SRC="tom.gif" BORDER=0> no border will be visible around the image named "tom.gif".

Bps (bits per second)   A measure of speed for how much data (measured in bits) can be transferred per second. A 14.4 modem can move 14,400 bits per second.

Browser   An application program used to view Internet content. Netscape Navigator and Microsoft Internet Explorer are two popular browsers.

Byte   Usually eight bits that represent a single character.

Cascading Style Sheets   An HTML extention that allows sophisticated formatting of HTML documents.

cgi-bin   The directory name, on a Web server, in which CGI scripts are stored. Some servers have one cgi-bin directory. Other servers provide a cgi-bin directory for each customer.

CGI Script   A small program, traditionally written in a scripting language like Perl, that is used to communicate between the server and browsers. This definition is usually extended to include small programs written in C, C++, or other compiled languages.

CGI (Common Gateway Interface)   A Protocol that describes how a Web server maintains a "dialog" with other pieces of software on the same machine.

Clickable Image Map   A map with a set of "hot spots." Clicking these hot spots will load another URL or execute a command.

Client-Side Image Map   Image maps where the map coordinates and URLs are downloaded to the client. This is a much more efficient and desirable arrangement than the older server-side image maps. The only drawback is not all browsers support client-side image maps.

Client   An application program that gets information from a server. There are many types of clients; Web browsers are good examples of clients.

Cookie   Persistent Client State HTTP Cookies are mechanisms that can be set and monitored by the server on the client side to track information about the client.

Domain Name   A unique name used to identify an Internet site. Common examples include **www.netscape.com**, **ftp.microsoft.com**, **vrml.sgi.com**, **www.svsu.edu**.

Drop Shadow   An effect commonly used to make it appear as though an image is casting a shadow onto an HTML page.

E-mail   Messages that are sent from one person to another electronically. These messages can include text, graphics, and audio information.

Ethernet   A common standard of connecting LANs.

FDDI (Fiber Distributed Data Interface)   A high-speed standard for transmitting data, approximately 10 times faster than ethernet.

Fire Wall   A hardware and software barrier constructed between a LAN and the Internet to provide security.

Font FACE   Helvetica, Arial, and Comic Sans MS are all examples of font faces. Or the FACE attribute that lets you specify a particular font used as <FONT FACE="Arial"> for example.

Frame   A special type of window defined by the FRAME tag.

FTP (File Transfer Protocol)   A method of moving files between two Internet sites.

GIF (Graphics Interchange Format)   A common image format. This file format can only represent 256 colors and is therefore best for representing line art or images with limited color range (unlike photographs or photo-realistic renderings). A GIF file may contain multiple images and therefore can be used for creating animations.

Hi_Res Image   A relative term, but usually reserved for images that are at least larger than 720x486.

Host   A computer that provides services to other computers on the network.

HTML Tags   The elements of HTML that are used to define page elements. HR, H1, and IMG are all examples of HTML tags.

HTML (HyperText Markup Language)   The language used to create Web pages. This language is made up of a set of TAGS used to define page elements and AT-TRIBUTES, which are applied to the tags.

HTTP (HyperText Transport Protocol)   The method used for moving hypertext files across the Internet. HTTP expects a server for distributing content and a browser for viewing it.

Hyperlink   A text or image reference that, when clicked by the user, loads an URL.

HyperText   Text or graphics that contain links to other words, documents, applications, or multimedia content.

Image Maps   A series of coordinates that define "hot areas" for the user to click.

Interlaced GIF   A GIF image file where the scan lines are stored in an alternating order, so that as the image is read it appears to fade in or get sharper. Do not use this option for saving GIF images that you will use for GIF animations.

Interlacing   The storage of image scan lines in an order other than the traditional top-to-bottom or bottom-to-top order.

Internet Explorer   A popular Web browser created by Microsoft.

Internet   The vast interconnected global network that provides the means for world-wide electronic communication.

Intranet   An internal network setup by an organization that uses the tools and protocols commonly found on the Internet for private use. Commonly used for corporate communication and other MIS functions.

IP Number   A number used to identify machines on the Internet. These are four-part numbers separated by periods. Even though many times "Domain Names" are used to connect to machines on the Internet, machines still do have, and must maintain their own, unique IP numbers.

ISDN (Integrated Services Digital Network) A method used to move digital data over phone lines at high speeds. Typically ISDN speeds are approximately 56,000 bits per second.

ISP (Internet service provider) A company or institution that provides Internet access and services.

Java Developer's Kit (JDK) A set of tools developed by Sun to help popularize the Java programming language.

Java A programming language invented by Sun Microsystems. Java includes a "byte-serve" interpreter on the client side that makes Java code portable across all platforms that run a Java-capable browser. Java applications (applets), can be written to perform almost any task from within the browser. Two limitations of applets are: their size must remain small or download time becomes extreme, and byte-code interpretation makes applets slow for computationally complex tasks.

JavaScript A scripting language that runs in a browser and extends the browsers capability for specific interactions.

JPEG An image format that provides user-definable compression. Best used on photo-realistic content. For line art see GIF.

LAN (Local Area Network) A computer network limited to a relatively small area (a room or an office building, for example).

Links Hyperlinks.

Looping The repeating of a series of frames. For GIF animations this is an attribute that can be explicitly built in during their construction.

MIDI An audio format that contains the "notes" of a song rather than digitized sound.

MIME (Multipurpose Internet Mail Extensions) The standard for attaching nontext files to e-mail. Attachments can include graphics, audio files, application programs, and so on. Besides e-mail, the MIME standard is used by Web servers to identify the files they are sending to clients.

MOD A format much like MIDI; it is a series of notes and instruments. In addition, Mod files include the samples of the instruments that are being used. Because of this, Mod files are much larger than MIDI files.

Part
VIII
App
B

Mosaic The original Web browser, this piece of software put a UI on the Internet.

MPEG A compression scheme used to compress audio and video content. MPEG requires significant processing power to both encode and decode the content.

Multicolumn Tag A Netscape extention that lets you create documents of multiple columns without using tables or frames.

Nested Frame A frame placed inside of an existing frame. Nesting frames makes creating sophisticated frame base documents easy.

Netiquette Internet etiquette.

Netscape Navigator The most popular Web browser. It was Netscape's willingness to embrace external technologies such as plug-ins that allowed many software companies to put diverse content on the Internet. Netscape's acceptance of Sun's Java programming language increased the flexibility and power of the browser model.

Newsgroup Discussion groups on USENET.

NIC (Networked Information Center) An office that handles information for a network. InterNIC is where domain names are registered and maintained.

Plug-In An application program designed to add functionality to a browser (or in a broader sense, any other application). A common example would be an application that lets you view images of a new format.

PNG A new image format that provides a superset of the GIF format's features, including full color and true transparency.

POP (Point of Presence) A location where an Internet connection can be established via dial-up phone lines.

PPP (Point-to-Point Protocol) This is a protocol that lets you use a phone line and a modem to establish a TCP/IP connection to the Internet. You can use this protocol to be assigned a temporary or permanent IP address.

Progressive JPEG A JPEG format where the image information is gradually downloaded. That is, a full-size, low-quality image initially appears, followed by successive passes that improve the image's quality. A progressive JPEG file takes no longer to download than a traditional JPEG file, and the end user can get a good idea of what the final image will look like with only 25 percent of the image downloaded.

QuickTime   An Apple multimedia format that can store images and audio.

Random Image Displayer   A CGI script that displays a series of images in a random order.

RealAudio   Either a plug-in or a format used to create and play streaming audio content.

Server-Side Image Map   An image map where the coordinate information and "URL" information is present on the server. This is an older technology and, for the most part, has been replaced by client-side image maps.

Server   Usually a computer and a software package that provides a service to other computers connected to the network. For Internet users, this can be any one of thousands of servers that provide Web content.

Shareware   Software distributed for a free trial period, usually lasting 30 days. If you find the software useful and want to continue using it beyond this trial period, you are required to pay the author the shareware fee. Shareware is not free unless expressly noted by the author.

ShockWave   A series of Macromedia plug-ins and associated formats that provide for the viewing and distribution of multimedia content.

SLIP (Serial line Internet Protocol)   This is a protocol that lets you use a phone line and a modem to establish a TCP/IP connection to the Internet. For the most part, this protocol is being replaced by PPP.

SPACER Tag   A Netscape extention that lets you add horizontal and vertical space within HTML documents.

Streaming Audio   Audio downloaded at a rate greater than or equal to the rate that it is being played. Theoretically, streaming audio can play indefinitely.

Sysop (system operator)   An individual responsible for the operation of a computer system or network.

T-1   A connection with a speed of 1,544,000 bits per second. This speed is still less than what is required to broadcast full-screen, full-color, full-motion video (30 frames per second) in an uncompressed format.

T-3   A connection with a speed of 44,736,000 bits per second. This speed is more than enough for full-motion video.

TCP/IP (Transmission Control Protocol/Internet Protocol)   This refers to the group of protocols used for transfer of data across the Internet; essential for all Internet connections.

Temporary Image   An image used as a placeholder when complex documents are being constructed and exact image dimensions are not known.

Tiled Image   A background image that repeats over and over. Sometimes, these images are carefully created so the seams between the repeated images are not visible.

Transparent Image   Images that contain transparency information. Currently, this is restrictive to GIF images where only one color can serve as the transparency color.

UNIX   A multiuser operating system with TCP/IP built in, important because it is the most common operating system for servers on the Internet.

URL (Uniform Resource Locator)   Used to give addresses to resources located across the World Wide Web. For example: **http://www.microsoft.com/help**.

Virtual Reality   Popularly defined as a world created and accessed by using computer technology.

W3C   The body that sets standards for the HyperText Markup Language (HTML).

WAN (wide area network)   A network that covers an area larger than a single building. Its usage is rather arbitrary. The difference between a LAN and a WAN is not always easily defined.

Wavelet   A new file format that provides storage of photo-realistic images. Most similar to JPEG.

Web   The World Wide Web.

WWW (World Wide Web)   Sometimes used to refer to the Internet as a whole—usually defined as the segment of the Internet accessible to browsers via HTTP servers.

What's on the CD

This Appendix briefly describes what you can find on the enclosed CD-ROM with this book. For more information on the contents, place the CD-ROM in your CD-ROM drive and open INDEX.HTM in your favorite browser. ■

Contents Overview

The CD-ROM included in this book contains several programs and utilities to add to your Web master bag of tricks. The CD includes:

- Several HTML Editors for Mac and Windows
- A GIF animation builder for Mac and Windows
- Image map creation tools
- Several audio editing programs
- The most popular archive and compression utilities for Mac and Windows
- The Java JDK
- Demonstration versions of several Macromedia products
- Dozens of plug-ins for your browser
- All the examples from this book

Loading the CD

The CD is designed to be used in conjunction with your Web browser. Simply pull down your browser's File menu and select Load File or its equivalent. Select the file index.htm, and it will load the beginning page, which then gives you the choices of software found on the CD. This CD supports frame-capable browsers and nonframe browsers alike. Once you have found a file you want to use, simply download it to your own hard drive (clicking a link) and then use a decompression utility to unarchive the contents if necessary.

Index

Check out Que® Books on the World Wide Web
http://www.mcp.com/que

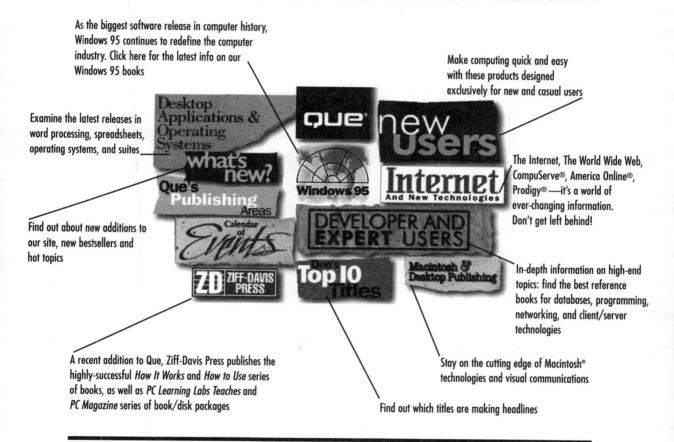

As the biggest software release in computer history, Windows 95 continues to redefine the computer industry. Click here for the latest info on our Windows 95 books

Examine the latest releases in word processing, spreadsheets, operating systems, and suites

Find out about new additions to our site, new bestsellers and hot topics

Make computing quick and easy with these products designed exclusively for new and casual users

The Internet, The World Wide Web, CompuServe®, America Online®, Prodigy® —it's a world of ever-changing information. Don't get left behind!

In-depth information on high-end topics: find the best reference books for databases, programming, networking, and client/server technologies

A recent addition to Que, Ziff-Davis Press publishes the highly-successful *How It Works* and *How to Use* series of books, as well as *PC Learning Labs Teaches* and *PC Magazine* series of book/disk packages

Stay on the cutting edge of Macintosh® technologies and visual communications

Find out which titles are making headlines

With 6 separate publishing groups, Que develops products for many specific market segments and areas of computer technology. Explore our Web Site and you'll find information on best-selling titles, newly published titles, upcoming products, authors, and much more.

- Stay informed on the latest industry trends and products available
- Visit our online bookstore for the latest information and editions
- Download software from Que's library of the best shareware and freeware

Complete and Return this Card
for a *FREE* Computer Book Catalog

Thank you for purchasing this book! You have purchased a superior computer book written expressly for your needs. To continue to provide the kind of up-to-date, pertinent coverage you've come to expect from us, we need to hear from you. Please take a minute to complete and return this self-addressed, postage-paid form. In return, we'll send you a free catalog of all our computer books on topics ranging from word processing to programming and the internet.

Mr. ☐   Mrs. ☐   Ms. ☐   Dr. ☐

Name (first) ☐☐☐☐☐☐☐☐☐☐☐   (M.I.) ☐   (last) ☐☐☐☐☐☐☐☐☐☐☐☐

Address ☐☐☐☐☐☐☐☐☐☐☐☐☐☐☐☐☐☐☐☐☐☐☐☐☐☐☐☐☐☐☐☐

☐☐☐☐☐☐☐☐☐☐☐☐☐☐☐☐☐☐☐☐☐☐☐☐☐☐☐☐☐☐☐☐

City ☐☐☐☐☐☐☐☐☐☐☐☐☐☐☐☐   State ☐☐   Zip ☐☐☐☐☐ ☐☐☐☐

Phone ☐☐☐ ☐☐☐ ☐☐☐☐   Fax ☐☐☐ ☐☐☐ ☐☐☐☐

Company Name ☐☐☐☐☐☐☐☐☐☐☐☐☐☐☐☐☐☐☐☐☐☐☐☐☐☐☐

E-mail address ☐☐☐☐☐☐☐☐☐☐☐☐☐☐☐☐☐☐☐☐☐☐☐☐☐☐☐

1. Please check at least (3) influencing factors for purchasing this book.

Front or back cover information on book .... ☐
Special approach to the content .... ☐
Completeness of content .... ☐
Author's reputation .... ☐
Publisher's reputation .... ☐
Book cover design or layout .... ☐
Index or table of contents of book .... ☐
Price of book .... ☐
Special effects, graphics, illustrations .... ☐
Other (Please specify): _____ ☐

2. How did you first learn about this book?

Saw in Macmillan Computer Publishing catalog .... ☐
Recommended by store personnel .... ☐
Saw the book on bookshelf at store .... ☐
Recommended by a friend .... ☐
Received advertisement in the mail .... ☐
Saw an advertisement in: _____ ☐
Read book review in: _____ ☐
Other (Please specify): _____ ☐

3. How many computer books have you purchased in the last six months?

This book only .... ☐   3 to 5 books..................... ☐
2 books.................. ☐   More than 5..................... ☐

4. Where did you purchase this book?

Bookstore .... ☐
Computer Store .... ☐
Consumer Electronics Store .... ☐
Department Store .... ☐
Office Club .... ☐
Warehouse Club .... ☐
Mail Order .... ☐
Direct from Publisher .... ☐
Internet site .... ☐
Other (Please specify): _____ ☐

5. How long have you been using a computer?

☐ Less than 6 months   ☐ 6 months to a year
☐ 1 to 3 years   ☐ More than 3 years

6. What is your level of experience with personal computers and with the subject of this book?

	With PCs	With subject of book
New	☐	☐
Casual	☐	☐
Accomplished	☐	☐
Expert	☐	☐

Source Code ISBN: 0-7897-0938-4

7. Which of the following best describes your job title?

Administrative Assistant .... ☐
Coordinator .... ☐
Manager/Supervisor .... ☐
Director .... ☐
Vice President .... ☐
President/CEO/COO .... ☐
Lawyer/Doctor/Medical Professional .... ☐
Teacher/Educator/Trainer .... ☐
Engineer/Technician .... ☐
Consultant .... ☐
Not employed/Student/Retired .... ☐
Other (Please specify): _____ ☐

8. Which of the following best describes the area of the company your job title falls under?

Accounting .... ☐
Engineering .... ☐
Manufacturing .... ☐
Operations .... ☐
Marketing .... ☐
Sales .... ☐
Other (Please specify): _____ ☐

Comments: _____
_____
_____

9. What is your age?

Under 20 .... ☐
21-29 .... ☐
30-39 .... ☐
40-49 .... ☐
50-59 .... ☐
60-over .... ☐

10. Are you:

Male .... ☐
Female .... ☐

11. Which computer publications do you read regularly? (Please list)

_____
_____
_____
_____
_____
_____
_____
_____
_____
_____
_____

Fold here and scotch-tape to mail.

Before using any of the software on this disc, you need to install the software you plan to use. See Appendix C, "What's on the CD-ROM," for directions. If you have problems with this CD-ROM, please contact Macmillan Technical Support at (317) 581-3833. We can be reached by e-mail at **support@mcp.com** or by CompuServe at **GO QUEBOOKS**.

Read this Before Opening Software

By opening this package, you are agreeing to be bound by the following:

This software is copyrighted and all rights are reserved by the publisher and its licensers. You are licensed to use this software on a single computer. You may copy the software for backup or archival purposes only. Making copies of the software for any other purpose is a violation of United States copyright laws. THIS SOFTWARE IS SOLD AS IS, WITHOUT WARRANTY OF ANY KIND, EITHER EXPRESSED OR IMPLIED, INCLUDING BUT NOT LIMITED TO THE IMPLIED WARRANTIES OF MERCHANTABILITY AND FITNESS FOR A PARTICULAR PURPOSE. Neither the publisher nor its dealers and distributors nor its licensers assume any liability for any alleged or actual damages arising from the use of this software. (Some states do not allow exclusion of implied warranties, so the exclusion may not apply to you.)

The entire contents of this disc and the compilation of the software are copyrighted and protected by United States copyright laws. The individual programs on the disc are copyrighted by the authors or owners of each program. Each program has its own use permissions and limitations. To use each program, you must follow the individual requirements and restrictions detailed for each. Do not use a program if you do not agree to follow its licensing agreement.